Will-o'-the-wisp

Will-o'-the-wisp

PETER THE PAINTER
and the anti-tsarist terrorists in Britain and Australia

F. G. CLARKE

Melbourne
OXFORD UNIVERSITY PRESS
Oxford Auckland New York

OXFORD UNIVERSITY PRESS

Oxford London Glasgow New York Toronto
Delhi Bombay Calcutta Madras Karachi
Kuala Lumpur Singapore Hong Kong Tokyo
Nairobi Dar es Salaam Cape Town
Melbourne Auckland
and associates in
Beirut Berlin Ibadan Mexico City Nicosia

National Library of Australia
Cataloguing-in-Publication data:

Clarke, F.G. (Frank G.), 1944-
Will-o'-the-Wisp.

Bibliography.
ISBN 0 19 554419 6

1. Terrorism - Great Britain
2. Terrorism - Australia.
I. Title.

364.1'55

OXFORD is a trade mark of Oxford University Press
Designed by Judy Hungerford
Typeset by Graphicraft Typesetters Limited, Hong Kong.
Printed by Nordica Printing Co.
Published by Oxford University Press, 7 Bowen Crescent, Melbourne

CONTENTS

PREFACE

Just over ten years ago, as a trainee archivist in the State Library of Western Australia, I was fortunate enough to be allocated the job of uncrating and listing the correspondence files selected for preservation from the huge holdings accumulated over many years in the office of the agent-general for Western Australia in the Strand, London. By and large, it was a dreary and uninspiring job. The files chosen for posterity seemed to concentrate on the impersonal and trivial side of the work done by an agent-general and tended to deal with such mundane concerns as the export potential of walking-sticks made from Western Australian native timbers, or the economic prospects of kangaroo skins in the English hat-manufacturing industry. Amongst a myriad of dry, sober-sided files, one stood out clearly as an exception, because it dealt with a person rather than a product. It was entitled 'The Ernest Dreger Case', and because it was so markedly different from the others, and comparatively slim into the bargain, I did more than just add it to the list; I read it. That marked the beginning of a ten-year obsession to find out all there was to know about the events so briefly and tantalizingly dealt with in that file. The chase has led from Western Australia to Canberra, and more recently to London. This book is the consummation of that curiosity which flared one hot summer's afternoon.

And yet, infuriatingly, the book raises as many questions as it answers. The protagonists are now all dead, and their descendants are unable to shed light on events about which their parents refused to speak. I have gone as far as I can with the evidence now available, and I have enjoyed the good fortune to be able to place those involved in the Australian end of the Ernest Dreger affair into a wider context in which their actions, aspirations and fears become more readily understandable when considering events in Russia and England which preceded the occurrences in Australia. This search for a wider framework has grown until it has become the main part of the story, but like so many things in Australian history, an adequate comprehension of what was happening in Europe is essential to understand why individuals acted as they did in Australia. Moreover, the incidents described as taking place in Russia and in

England are now part of Australian social history, and their legacy and impact will be traced in the following chapters.

I am indebted to so many people that it is difficult to know just where to begin, but it is certainly true to say that without the generosity and friendship of Donald Rumbelow this work most probably would have remained an unfinished manuscript. Donald Rumbelow unearthed and secured for future scholars the files of the City of London police force dealing with the Houndsditch murders and the siege of Sidney Street. His own stimulating and successful book on the Houndsditch affair was the first published account to make use of this material. Rather than guarding these records with the proprietal jealousy that one often finds in academics, Donald Rumbelow generously made them available, and we spent many an enjoyable hour in close discussion of the case and its ramifications. For his kindness, helpfulness and genial hospitality, I am heavily in his debt.

I am grateful also to my own university, which has supported me generously in my research into the background for this book, and which gave me a year's sabbatical leave to follow up and complete the research in England. Like most writers on historical topics I owe a great deal collectively to the assistance I received from the staffs of the Guildhall Records Office, the Public Records Office, and the British Museum in England; the State Library of Western Australia; the Australian Archives in Canberra and Western Australia; and the Central Army Records Office in Victoria. My thanks also go to the Corporation of London, the West Australian State Archives and Donald Rumbelow for the use of their photographs.

I have received nothing but encouragement from my friends and colleagues, Edith Mary Johnston, George Liik, Trevor McClaughlin, George Raudzens, Portia Robinson and Robin Walker.

Mrs Jadviga Raudzens translated letters in a variety of Eastern European languages which had lain ignored for more than fifty years in the files of the Western Australian Police Department; and the descendants of Ernest Dreger both in Western Australia and in New South Wales helped me in every way they could.

My mother, Mrs Norma Clarke, undertook the difficult task of turning my almost indecipherable handwriting into a typescript; Mrs Cora Duim transposed this via the word processor. And my wife and family have shown forbearance above and beyond the call of duty by putting up with a husband and father's obsession with a group of terrorist fanatics, and in supporting and encouraging rather than resenting the time spent in my study.

If the book possesses any merit, it belongs to these people. Its many faults belong to nobody but myself.

F.G. CLARKE, 1983

1
PRELUDE
TO
TERROR

The custom of viewing Russia as a homogeneous and powerful monolith is not new. From the time of the first Napoleon, Russia constituted a major factor in the European balance of power; a huge reservoir of manpower and destructive potential that had only to be mobilized to place under threat the continued existence of most of western Europe. Accordingly, the tsar of All the Russias was a person to be respected and placated. When he spoke, he did so with the weight of the countless millions of his loyal subjects behind him. The sheer immensity and geographical unity of the tsar's empire made Russia a power to be reckoned with, in Europe, in Asia, in America and in the Middle East.

Ironically, it was the size of the Russian empire that was both the source of its strength and its greatest weakness. For the tsar's domain was ethnically heterogeneous and included numerous subject races, each with its own language, culture and traditional territories. The people who later composed the independent nation - states of Latvia, Estonia and Lithuania - were all subsumed within the Russian empire at the close of the nineteenth century, and although they were minorities within the whole of Russian society, they were nonetheless significant national minorities. Among the most important and substantial of these, at least insofar as the background to this story is concerned, was the Jews.

All the national groups suffered from varying degrees of Russification, but it was the Jews who were interfered with most grievously. As the nineteenth century progressed, the situation of Jews in Russia declined alarmingly. They were subjected to extraordinary vicissitudes during the reign of Tsar Nicholas I (1825-55) when they were forced to move into the huge and infamous ghetto the Pale of Settlement, which extended from the Baltic to the Black Sea. Once resettled, they endured a continual series of pressures designed to turn them into 'ordinary' Russians. The tsars tended towards anti-semitism, and Nicholas I seemed resolved to attempt the spiritual and physical destruction of the Jewish people in his empire.[1]

One of the most malevolent methods of fighting ethnic obduracy and advancing Russification - which also affected the other national minorities, though not so severely - was the Army Recruiting Ordinance of 1827. Its ostensible aim was to equalize military duty for all estates in the empire, but it proved to be especially discriminatory against the Jews. Jewish communities were instructed to secure a quota of recruits for the army from youths aged between twelve and twenty-five. The ratio was fixed for the Jews at ten recruits per thousand of population, and the local communes were responsible for selecting the correct number of recruits and delivering them to the authorities. Failure to produce the allocated number of recruits meant heavy fines and possible recruitment of the commune leaders themselves. William Fishman has outlined graphically the degrading treatment suffered by these young recruits to the tsar's army. A Jewish soldier could be forced to serve in the army for thirty-one years, and very few of them ever survived to return to their families. It became customary for Jews to recite the prayers for the dead over the young conscripts - most were never seen again. They were marched to recruiting centres and from there despatched to their respective units. A conscious policy of Russification was followed while they were in the army, which was designed to break down any separate ethnic consciousness. As they marched to units all over the Russian empire they were billeted perforce on Gentile families. There the recruits either ate non-kosher food or they starved. The roads were strewn with the bodies of Jewish recruits who never reached their units. Once arrived, even worse awaited them: a forced christening and reception into the Greek Orthodox religion. Resistance to such aculturation was suppressed brutally.

The stubborn, who resisted the holy water, were in succession flogged, forced to eat pork and salted fish, then deprived of water. Exercises in religious brainwashing were performed by the holy fathers. Those who persisted ended up in military hospitals where they died. In the many attempts at genocide prior to the holocaust, none were so manifestly depraved as this exercise in the moral and physical destruction of Jewish children. [2]

There were other attempts to de-culturalize the Jews: by interfering in the education of their children; by enforcing the use of Russian as the language of education, business and commerce; and by burning most of the books published in Hebrew. Finally, there was the systematic uprooting and forced transference of entire communities to the Pale of Settlement. In Courland, one of the Baltic provinces, for example, all Jews not born there were forced to leave. Any Jews who failed to register themselves in a municipality within six months were liable for military conscription or for deportation to Siberia. Once driven within the Pale, Jews - with a few unimportant exceptions - were not permitted to leave again. Similar restrictions on freedom of movement also affected members of the other national minorities who were forced to carry internal passports if they moved outside their own districts.

Moreover, in addition to these afflictions, the Jews in Russia suffered appallingly from anti-semitic pogroms throughout the nineteenth century and up until 1917, when the Jews were freed by the revolution and allowed to move into Russia proper if they so desired.

The wretchedness and tribulations endured by the Jews in Russia were worse than those undergone by any other minority, but they highlight in the starkest way the type of policies that were also applied, though in a modified form, to those other national minorities that also found themselves reluctant subjects of the tsars. The Baltic peoples similarly suffered from Russian de-culturalization programmes and the proscribing of their languages. They were relegated to the lowest social level in their homelands, and, like the Jews, they developed a fierce hatred of the tsars and everything they represented. Russification programmes kindled nationalistic reactions in both the Jews and the Letts, the two peoples around whom this story revolves, and as the autocratic regime persisted a stubborn and occasionally violent reaction occurred in which the oppressed turned on their persecutors; officially sanctioned brutality and repression created a counter-wave of equal brutality and aggression. The tsarist regime was autocratic, hereditary, aristocratic and regulated; the reaction it generated proved to be at various times democratic, socialistic, revolutionary and anarchistic.

By the end of the nineteenth century anti-tsarist opposition tended to fall into one of two patterns. Neither excluded the other, and many of those involved played both roles at different stages of their revolutionary careers. Firstly, there occurred a proliferation of secret anti-government organizations dedicated to the protection of their members and sometimes to the violent overthrow of the existing regime. These groups covered every possible ethnic and philosophical or political persuasion, from the Jewish Bund to the anarcho-communism of the Lettish League or the Lettish Social Democratic Party, but they shared a detestation of the existing system and a determination to change it. Occasionally, they worked together against the tsarist authorities, but more often the opposition remained a philosophically and politically diverse conglomeration of distrustful and squabbling societies, each pursuing its own limited objectives in complete isolation from its potential allies within the broad spectrum of opposition. The government exploited these divisions in an attempt to set one group of revolutionaries against another. In this endeavour it was often successful.

Moreover, for the ethnic minorities life within the Russian empire could become quite intolerable even if one did not come to the attention of the police as a suspected subversive. In such a police state any special interest by the authorities in the affairs of a revolutionary often resulted in flight abroad.

The considerations favouring a decision to emigrate were twofold: emigration was an escape from a way of life that had for many become unendurable; and it meant deliverance from persecution and the restrictions of an oppressive autocratic system of government together with the hope of a better life for the emigrant and ultimately for his family. Furthermore, emigration was also a way out for those who were beginning to feel hemmed in by the huge population growth of the nineteenth century. To an oppressed and impoverished peasantry the sex act amounted to the only pleasure in a short and brutish life. Between 1820 and 1880, for example, the Jewish population in Russia and Poland increased by 150 per cent from just over one and a half million to four million,[3] and by 1914 the populace of imperial Russia included some six million Jewish subjects.[4] Such fecundity was not limited to the Jews. In the same period to 1880 the non-Jewish population of tsarist Russia increased by 87 per cent. Thus it seems probable that population pressure alone would have constituted a major push-factor in any decision to emigrate, without the additional incentive of intolerable political repression. The effect of such push-factors reinforcing one another can be seen in the emigration levels following the wave of pogroms after the assassination of Tsar Alexander II by terrorists in March 1881. Within a year 225,000 Jewish families emigrated from Russia. Most of them intended to settle in the United States, but a substantial minority sought immediate refuge in a land much closer to their former home. It was the beginning of the Eastern Europeanization of the docks and their environs in the East End of London.

Great Britain had become an important staging area in the campaign against the tsar quite early in the nineteenth century. In 1853, the exiled Russian political thinker Alexander Herzen produced the first pamphlets published by his Russian Free Press in London. In 1857 Herzen and his helpers produced the first issue of the famous Russian paper the *Bell*, which was smuggled into Russia and eagerly read even - according to rumour - by the tsar himself.[5] Many Russian *émigrés* who still wished to continue the revolutionary struggle chose to live in England which had a dual tradition of harbouring refugees and of political tolerance. Furthermore, many of these *émigrés* had families still in Russia. They hoped to obtain work in Britain and to remit sufficient funds to ensure a reunion in England before proceeding as a group to the United States. England, however, provided no easy bulwark against adversity, and the refugees faced hardships and privations in Britain that must, on occasions, have made life in Russia seem almost endurable.

On arrival in England most Russian refugees were usually poor and down at heel. They were disembarked at the London docks with their belongings and left to their own resources. Needless to say, many became victims of the predators who have always bedevilled large-scale emigration schemes, and the refugees were fortunate if they found their way into the huge refugee catchment area of London's East End with their money and meagre belongings intact. Unless they knew friends or relatives who could protect them until they were settled the refugees had to find lodgings, food and some sort of employment as quickly as

possible. A few lucky ones obtained a place in the special Jewish hostel
where they were fed and lodged for a fortnight while they established themselves in work and accommodation. Non-Jews had little organized assistance and were forced to make the best of things on their own. Rooms were difficult to obtain. The East End had become the focus of this large and continuing migration, and the local English and Irish population slowly found itself forced out of the area, which deteriorated rapidly. Landlords rack-rented the run-down tenement buildings to the desparate and poverty - stricken refugees. The housing problem was exacerbated by the presence of thousands of transmigrants in London who competed for limited accommodation with permanent residents. The figures for immigration and transmigration give some indication of the pressures on a decaying urban environment by this rush of new, albeit in some cases temporary, settlement. Many European emigrants travelled to the United States via England. The shipping lines engaged in price-cutting wars that made England a magnet for would-be emigrants. In the decade ending in 1901, for example, over 800,000 continental transmigrants travelled via England to their final destinations. Many of these people stayed for comparatively long periods, either to work and save money or to await the arrival of relatives and friends before continuing their journey. The flow of permanent settlers, however, fluctuated annually between a high of 6000 and a low of 2000.[6]

Overcrowding in the East End became endemic because most *émigrés* were reluctant to move to other parts of the United Kingdom. The great majority of the refugees came from urban or village environments and were not peasants. They included such a preponderance of Jews that 'immigrant' and 'Jew' became synonyms in the East End. The Russian administration had made it almost impossible for Jews to own land as farmers or to engage in traditional rural occupations. Cities, therefore, were familiar to them, and the attractions of London were unrivalled. A recent writer has shown that at any time between 1881 and 1905, 60 per cent of all foreigners in England might be found in London, its suburbs and the Home Counties.[7] Such a concentration meant that in the East End the newly arrived refugee found a society to which he was accustomed. It was a place where people could understand him, where he would find his language spoken, his compatriots in exile as neighbours, his normal dietary requirements both religious and customary adequately catered for, and understanding, sympathetic companionship from fellow *émigrés* who had a common bond of shared hardship and hostility towards the Russian government. To venture out of the East End brought him into the strange and frightening environment of Anglo-Saxon or Anglo-Celtic society, where language and cultural differences barred his progress, to say nothing of the traditional British contempt for foreigners of any sort.[8] Not surprisingly, most *émigrés* remained within the familiar East End environment.

Life in the East End was a constant struggle for survival. At the end of the nineteenth century industrialization was only just beginning in Russia, and few of the emigrants had any experience of factories and generally lacked the necessary capital to open up businesses in their adopted home. Those with money tended to sink it into property which they rack-rented. There were usually several levels of sub-letting involved, and severe overcrowding was the norm rather than the exception. The majority of refugees found themselves forced into the old traditional handcraft occupations of tailoring, bootmaking, locksmithing, watch repairing, dressmaking, and cigarette rolling. Since these jobs were done mainly in factories outside the East End, the *émigré* tradesman was usually in direct competition with large industrial concerns. His supply of work naturally tended to fluctuate as seasonal demand rose and fell, and because such a large pool of unemployed labour existed in the East End community, the wages paid were very low and the hours of work exceedingly long. The experience of most newly arrived refugees was that work was difficult to obtain and harder to keep. If they tried to find work outside the East End, they ran up against the barrier of trade union restrictions designed to protect the livelihoods of English labourers from the threat of cheap continental labour.

Most refugee workers began their career in the clothing industry. They worked for several weeks as 'greeners' for food and lodging only, until they developed sufficient skill in the specialized function allotted them to increase their output to a level at which they were entitled to a meagre daily wage. The East End sweatshops generally operated on a system of rigid specialization of function. No one made a whole garment or an entire shoe or boot. Traditional craftsmanship of that sort was too slow. The entire manufacturing process was broken down into stages, and each stage was allotted to one person who performed nothing but that task. Thus people became specialist seamstresses, or tailors' pressers, or boot clickers or button sewers. Only in this way could an employer attain an output sufficiently high to compete with industrialized clothes manufacturers or shoemakers. Although the employers in these situations worked their employees unmercifully, they themselves were not the bloated exploiters they were accused of being. Generally speaking, they worked harder and longer for less return than did their employees, but there was always the chance that with luck they could begin to claw their way up to the bourgeois levels of society. Very few of them were ultimately successful, most failed and slipped down again into the mass of wage earners. Each small recession in the tailoring or dressmaking business sent scores of small employers to the wall, but there were always others prepared to hire a few sewing machines and take a chance in the hope of making good.

In a society based upon such a system, the standard of living was appallingly low, at least by English standards. Of course, these refugees had escaped from a society where brutality and degradation were commonplace, and where a level of mere subsistence was difficult to obtain. Once in England, such people continued for the most part to accept a very low standard of living, for two main reasons. Firstly, they knew no other, and wages in the East End allowed little leeway or luxury above maintaining existence. But secondly, many *émigrés* had left their families behind in Russia, and sent them as much as they could spare from the pittance they earned. A contemporary account of 1906 indicates that some Englishmen at least were aware that the precarious frugality of the immigrants in London stemmed from necessity and affection rather than meanness and avarice:

Yet, after all, who can blame them? If they live on a piece of black rye bread and an onion, or a piece of fish fried in olive oil by way of a luxury, they at least know that their frugality and economy will, by-and-by, enable them to alleviate the wants of their old people at home or bring some young and cherished relative out of the 'land of bondage'.

How constantly these voluntary and involuntary Russian exiles manage, through sheer industry and economy, to send remittances to their friends, may be inferred from the fact that nearly a million of roubles is yearly sent to Russia and Poland by the Ghetto Bank of Whitechapel. Drafts from five roubles upwards are issued by this bank, and for the convenience of customers it is open 'till ten o'clock at night, with the exception of the Jewish Sabbath. It reopens on Saturday evening, and it works all Sunday. It transacts every kind of business connected with banking, shipping, emigration and immigration. It has agents in every important town of Russia, and in all the provinces of the empire, including, of course, Poland. And it has special agents not only in Russia, but also at Bremen, Hamburg and Rotterdam . . . It is never without a customer. Every minute of the day is occupied by answering all kinds of queries in Russian, Polish, German, Dutch, and other languages, and in changing coins and paper money. [9]

There was, however, another dimension to refugee activities in London in addition to the struggle for survival or the rescue of friends and relatives still in Russia. London also proved to be a useful base for the planning and implementation of revolutionary and terrorist activities directed against the tsarist regime in the homelands, especially during and after the abortive revolutions in Russia and the Baltic provinces during the troubles of 1905.

The tsar's empire came close to crumbling in 1905. The war against the rising power of Japan for Manchuria and Korea had proved a costly fiasco, and caused many professional military and revolutionary strategists to re-evaluate the military worth of the huge conscript armies and the navy; they fought badly, they mutinied and seemed ripe for revolution. At the same time, a series of unco-ordinated and apparently unplanned strikes, assassinations and mutinies in the Baltic provinces and in

Russia itself directly attacked the power of autocracy. It was a strangely
assorted combination of bourgeois and revolutionary organizations that
temporarily came together in opposition to the tsar. On 30 October the
tsar capitulated and through the October Manifesto granted a state duma
(a council of state elected on a broad suffrage) together with a new
constitution and guarantees of freedom of speech and assembly. The
revolutionaries regarded this as merely cosmetic tinkering and of trifling
importance; they wished to see a major change in the structure of the
state and the transfer of executive power into the hands of the workers.
The manifesto, however, did satisfy the bourgeois reformists who had
become alarmed by the strikes and revolutionary activities that had
broken out all over the Russian empire. As a result they drew back, and
instead of a full-scale revolution leading to the ultimate triumph of the
workers' self-elected leaders, the result was failure, disappointment and
eventually the clamping down of an unrestrained white terror* throughout the Russian empire. In the Baltic provinces, where nationalism and
revolution had become indistinguishable, all suspected opponents (and
their families) of the regime were subjected to a ferocious assault by the
reorganized forces of tsarist reaction.

In twelve months from April 1905 more than 14,000 people lost their
lives. A thousand were hanged and more than 7000 were imprisoned or
exiled. Those imprisoned or dealt with by military courts were often
sickeningly tortured. Jacob Peters, for example, who had been an
agitator and organizer for the Social Democrats in the Riga shipyards,
had his fingernails torn out with pincers. He could count himself lucky
that the authorities had not realized what a prominent role he had played
during the troubles in Riga. The fate of those who were suspected of
taking a major part in the revolution was unenviable. Peters told of a
comrade who was arrested and tortured with him: not only did this poor
wretch have his fingernails torn out but the prison authorities also
punctured his eardrums and finally tore off his genitals.[10] Maria
Spiridonova, a female revolutionary, commented that women as well as
men suffered under this reaction. She described how in her own region
the local landowner returned with a party of cossacks and personally led
punitive expeditions to eighteen villages. The rebel ring-leaders were
taken away, and wholesale floggings with the knout were then dealt out
to the rest of the men and women of the village. Often the peasants' huts
and their granaries were burned. According to Spiridonova's evidence:
'After his departure the invariable appearance of the villages was that
which we generally associate with Bulgarian villages after they have been
devastated by the Turks.'[11] The authorities empowered military field

---

* In terms of Russian politics in this period there existed three primary colours repre-
senting the major political divisions. Firstly, there were the revolutionaries belonging to
various organizations including the socialist parties known collectively as 'reds';
secondly, the anarchists who operated under the black flag; and thirdly the supporters
of the Romanov dynasty, known as the 'whites'.

courts martial to dispense 'justice' in the areas affected by revolutionary disturbances, with the result that it is impossible to calculate accurately the death toll. These courts martial carried out their sentences of death – usually by hanging or shooting – within twenty-four hours of a suspected revolutionary appearing before them. Their procedures were summary in the extreme. Field courts martial took place in about a hundred localities in the empire from Vladivostok to the Baltic. Warsaw recorded the highest number of such killings with fifty-nine executions, closely followed by Riga with fifty-seven.

In addition to this official terror, the revitalized tsarist regime hit back at its enemies in an unofficial, though not unanticipated, fashion. Hundreds of pogroms swept the villages and townships of the Pale of Settlement. Police and troops assisted the mobs of rioters involved in these convulsions in which hundreds of people were killed and thousands were wounded. The tsarist functionaries attempted to channel the violence and to direct attention from their own failures and shortcomings to the historic scapegoats of Eastern Europe. The supporters of these pogroms came from the ranks of impoverished gentry, artisans, and the bourgeoisie – in short, all those who had felt threatened by the strikes and the revolutionary movements of 1905. Jews were prominent in many insurrectionary groups, and in addition the underground revolutionary Jewish Bund organization spread throughout the Pale and co-operated closely with the anarchists, social revolutionaries, nihilists and social democrats. Moreover, it was widely believed in official circles that Jews were in league with freemasonry to overthrow the state.[12] This was the period when that notorious forgery *The Protocols of the Elders of Zion* was launched in Russia, possibly with a view to convincing Tsar Nicholas II that Jews and freemasons were undermining his throne.*

The impact of such officially sanctioned repression in the Baltic provinces and the pogroms in the Pale of Settlement was twofold. There was, as we have already seen, a huge flood of refugees who abandoned their homes for sanctuaries outside Russia. But there was also a stiffening of resolve amongst those revolutionary bodies opposed to tsarism, and a new willingness to embrace terrorism as a legitimate weapon to be used against autocratic and bourgeois opponents, not only in Russia but throughout the world.[13] England was not destined to escape the effects of this resolve. Nor was Australia.

Britain had always provided an important refuge for opponents of the tsar, and many of the anti-tsarist organizations used England as a rendezvous for devising future campaigns. It was the headquarters, for

---

* *The Protocols of the Elders of Zion* purported to be a Jewish blueprint for world domination and for the overthrow of all legitimate Christian governments. This objective was to be achieved by undermining the moral fibre of Christians and by financing revolutionary organizations dedicated to the destruction of existing political structures. The forgery has since then provided the theoretical backbone of European anti-semitism, which culminated in the Nazi holocaust.

example, of the underground railway which smuggled large quantities of forbidden newspapers, pamphlets and proclamations into Russia. England was also used as a place to assemble shipments of arms and ammunition, which were then conveyed surreptitiously to Russia when needed. During the winter of 1904 the British socialist S.G. Hobson participated directly in the smuggling of 6000 Browning revolvers. The guns were hidden in barrels of lard and shipped through Riga, Russia's main Baltic port.[14] Another, similar episode involved the secret cache of firearms purchased and assembled in London during 1905 for shipment to the revolutionaries. There were 15,000 rifles, two and a half million cartridges, 2500 revolvers, and three tons of explosives. The SS *John Grafton* was chartered to convey these stores to Russia, but most of the cargo was lost as the ship concluded a Gilbertian voyage by running aground before the bulk of its contraband cargo could be landed.[15] England, therefore, was more than just a haven for those who wished to escape tsarism and start a new life. It was also the nerve centre of a network of revolutionary groups and terrorist organizations that were resolved to find solutions to the difficulties in their own countries by force, and at the same time to deal ruthlessly with any representatives of capitalist, bourgeois society who opposed them.

The debate over the primacy of moral or physical force in opposing repressive regimes has a long history in anti-tsarist activities and pre-dates the troubles of 1905. Organizations developed which formalized the varying points of view in this dispute, and because members of these associations were destined to play a major part in the following events the distinctions must be made clear.

It is sufficient for this purpose to divide the main revolutionary groups into three major categories, though the reality was far more obscure than such a simplified division implies.

Anarchists were always an important group in the campaign against tsarist repression, and they were involved in some spectacular feats of terrorism and 'propaganda by the deed'. There were many sympathizers with the libertarian philosophy espoused by the anarchists, but by its very nature it was a belief that made a tight and disciplined approach to organization and activity almost impossible. Convinced anarchists tended to be individualists, although a small group did accept the necessity for formalized working arrangements for the duration of the revolutionary struggle. At this stage of the revolutionary campaign, however, anarchists tended to operate in an unco-ordinated fashion eschewing the discipline and direction of the more rigidly regulated parties. They did achieve a degree of infamy throughout Europe for their resort to violence and acts of individual terrorism. The myth of the Black International, said to be a secret organization of anarchists that directed its activities against the forces of law and order in all states and countries of Europe, was popularized by the sensationalist press, and there seems little doubt that anarchists received much of the blame for atrocities that

ought more fairly to have been attributed to the Social Democrats or the
Socialist Revolutionaries. European newspapers tended to blame outrages
on anarchists rather than the other groups in the years before the First
World War.

Near the turn of the century the two main revolutionary bodies each
established party structures to replace the more amorphous 'circles' of
earlier years. The Marxists in 1898 founded the Russian Social Democratic Labour Party. In 1902 the non-Marxists established the Socialist
Revolutionary Party. Both these parties were like icebergs and possessed
small lawful organizations which maintained some degree of legally
permitted political activity throughout the last years of the empire. They
also, however, had large clandestine structures which were hidden from
public scrutiny and engaged in the unlawful fermenting of revolution and
terror.

At this stage a crucial clarification must be made because there are
two different kinds of terror, and the two parties differed markedly from
one another in their respective attitudes to each. Terrorism as a means of
seizing power, as a weapon in the revolutionary struggle, was known as
'individual terrorism'. Attempted assassinations of prominent aristocratic figures like the tsar and his family, or repressive generals, chiefs of
police, and bourgeois politicians were considered to be legitimate
weapons by the Socialist Revolutionary Party which established a large
battle organization within the party to plan and carry out such activities.
The battle organization was responsible for hundreds of murders of
middle-level government officials after 1902, in addition to several
spectacular attempts on the life of the tsar and the murder of the Russian
Premier, Stolypin, in 1911.

The Marxist Social Democrats, on the other hand, rejected this tactic
not for moral reasons but merely for practical and political considerations. This remained the public stance of the Russian Social Democratic
Party towards acts of individual terrorism *per se*, though like the other
two groups the Social Democrats believed in forcing the bourgeoisie to
pay for the revolution by robbing banks, department stores, post-offices,
and any other likely sources of government or capitalist money. All the
terrorist groups relied heavily on 'expropriations' to finance their
activities, and it was because of this that certain individuals came
eventually to the attention of the English and Australian police
forces.

The second variety of terrorism did not lead to major divisions
between the Social Democrats and the Socialist Revolutionaries, although
it was the cause of a wholesale breach between these two parties and the
anarchists. This was mass terrorism as a method of revolutionary
government, as a means of retaining power and of governing the masses
after the overthrow of the old regime. By this method, terrorism was to
be applied not to particular individuals who were guilty of forbidden or
criminal acts, but to whole categories of people selected by reason of

some common attribute, such as land-ownership or an income above a certain level, and regardless of their individual behaviour or activities. Such terror was to be inflicted on the old ruling and bourgeois classes in the years after the Revolution in 1917, and with the full agreement of both Social Democrats and Socialist Revolutionaries who shared in the government after Lenin came to power. The anarchists were totally opposed philosophically to the concept of mass terror as a legitimate instrument of government, and they were among the first to suffer its consequences after the Revolution when they were suppressed bloodily as opponents of the new regime by the Bolsheviks. In 1905, however, the three groups shared a detestation of the tsarist autocracy and a readiness to resort to violence to hasten its demise.

With the three main anti-tsarist groups all endorsing one form or other of individual terrorism, the decades immediately prior to the revolution of 1917 were a time when world opinion was staggered by a number of terrorist atrocities both inside and outside Russia. Many refugees took their political convictions with them and violently attacked what they regarded as bourgeois elements in their hosts' societies. International terrorism was as well known before 1914 as it is in the 1980s. This partial chronology of terrorist activities in these early years gives some idea of the scope and nature of the campaign of individual terrorism. In 1878 there were two attempts to shoot the German kaiser and an attempt to stab the king of Italy. The following year there were two attempts on the life of the tsar, followed by a successful assassination the next year. In 1880 shots were fired at the king and queen of Spain. In 1886 a bomb killed eight policemen at a meeting of anarchists in the Haymarket in Chicago. In 1890 the assassination of General Seliverstoff, formerly head of the Ochrana (tsarist secret police) took place. Two years later six anarchists were arrested at Walsall in England and were sentenced to long terms in jail for manufacturing bombs. In the same year the revenge killing of the mayor of Chicago occurred, an attempt was made to blow up the Spanish parliament and four French policemen were killed in a bomb explosion. In 1893 at Barcelona a bomb was thrown from the gallery of the Lices Theatre, killing twenty people. In Paris an anarchist threw a bomb into the French parliament which exploded in the air and wounded sixty people. In 1894 an anarchist blew himself to pieces while placing a bomb designed to blow up the Royal Observatory at Greenwich in England. In France the French President, Carnot, was stabbed to death by a young anarchist in a crime described by former English Prime Minister Lord Salisbury to the House of Lords as an enterprise which had been confected in safety in Britain by foreign anarchists.[16] Two years later the Empress Elizabeth of Austria was assassinated, and in 1900 King Humbert of Italy was stabbed to death. The following year President McKinley of the United States was shot by a Polish anarchist at a reception in Buffalo. In every year from 1901 to 1917 a host of Russian dignitaries was killed, ranging from the tsar's uncle, the Grand Duke Sergius, and the Prime Minister Stolypin, through sundry generals and government functionaries, down to policemen and prison warders. And it should be remembered that all these acts of individual terrorism, whether effected by Social Democrats, Socialist Revolutionaries, anarchists or unbalanced individuals, tended to be blamed on 'anarchists' in the press, without much regard for the fine distinctions such incendiary and exotic organizations made between themselves. Like all oversimplifications, such an analysis did contain a grain of truth, and its rejection by the London police was to obscure the essentially political nature of such crimes and lead to a situation where needless deaths and great destruction would occur.

Amongst the refugees who fled from Russia after 1905 were many who had decided to carry on the struggle from abroad. Some settled in Stockholm, others in France and Spain, others in the United States, and a not insignificant number selected Britain as their base of operations. The Russian authorities had already taken precautions to combat the activities of such *émigrés* and to keep a close watch on their plans for future operations. This watching-brief was entrusted to an official secret organization, established to oversee and report on the illegal machinations of dissidents both within Russia and in exile. Known as the Ochrana, these secret police soon developed a range of covert activities. Where possible, they infiltrated their own agents into the dissident political organizations in Russia, and when this proved impossible they subverted existing members. In this devious and exceedingly dangerous game they enjoyed considerable success. The leader of the Socialist Revolutionaries' battle organization in charge of assassination and expropriation planning was in the pay of the Ochrana. They thus received ample warning of all attempts on the life of the tsar and the lives of other high officials in plenty of time to forestall them. The parliamentary leader of Lenin's Social Democrats in the duma was also an Ochrana agent, and the chief of police wrote his speeches for him, or rather rewrote those sent to the parliamentarian by Lenin. Joseph Stalin was reputed to be a police spy, as were many of the foremost revolutionaries such as the trade union leader Father Gabon.[17]

These infiltrators were successful because the Ochrana had been established on a professional basis early in the twentieth century. Agents in the opposition groups were encouraged to rise as high in them as they could, even if this meant actual involvement in crimes and assassination attempts. Without such close involvement, the agent could not rise high in the revolutionary organizations. The Ochrana protected its agents from arrest and punishment when outrages were investigated and arrests were imminent, or else it arranged convenient 'escapes' for its own people from police custody, thereby enhancing their reputations as dyed-in-the-wool revolutionaries. Gerasimov, the head of the St Petersburg Ochrana, for example, maintained up to 150 such agents inside the revolutionary parties at all levels of the organizations. Thus when revolutionaries fled abroad or went into hiding outside Russia after 1905, agents of the Ochrana went with them.

Nor was this the only way in which the tsarist authorities maintained their surveillance on revolutionaries skulking abroad. As early as 1883 the Ochrana had established a foreign agency attached to the Imperial Russian Consulate in Paris. When terrorists fled to neighbouring countries they quickly came to the attention of the foreign agency which operated against refugee political organizations in Switzerland and England as well as in France, and also at times in Germany, Austria and elsewhere in Europe. The foreign agency's methods closely approximated those used by the parent organization at home, and agents were infiltrated into the revolutionary organizations with the intention of keeping the Russian authorities fully informed about the *émigrés'* plans for future action. At the same time, they acted as *agents provocateurs*, inciting the exiles to political violence and informing the local police. In this way they brought the revolutionaries into disrepute with their host societies and ensured that many potentially dangerous activists were locked away in foreign prisons. Several of the so-called anarchist outrages in these years can be ascribed to the work of *agents provocateurs*. Ronald Hingley describes one episode in Paris where a Russian police spy wormed his way into the confidence of an *émigré* group where he posed as an apostle of extreme violence. He persuaded his new comrades to plot the assassination of Tsar Alexander III from French territory, and he even provided funds from the foreign agency to help them build a bomb factory in the Forest of Raincy. At a well-judged moment the *agent* disappeared, and the other plotters were all arrested by the French police. This individual later became the head of the foreign agency.[18]

The work of such men was made easier by the violent character of many *émigrés*. Frequently they were faced with the prospect of working extraordinarily long hours at exhausting occupations merely to stay alive. In such situations their revolutionary ardour was in danger of being dissipated altogether. An exiled revolutionary needed spare time to read, to continue his political education, to engage in covert activities against the repressive elements in Russia and in the host country. To many such as these, earning a living was a distraction. It was easy for such people to justify an existence based on 'expropriation' as a politically desirable one. They slipped quickly into illegal activities, and any action that could be illustrated as being directed against the bourgeois owners of capital was regarded as revolutionary.[19]

England was not destined to escape the effects of the agents planted by the foreign agency. Sir Melville Macnaghten, the former head of Scotland Yard, alleged in 1914 that the attempt to blow up the Greenwich Observatory in 1894 was probably the result of work by a police spy on the feebleminded enthusiast Bourdin, who blew himself to pieces in the process. Bourdin was a foreigner, which perhaps explains Macnaghten's cavalier account of the incident.

There was at that time an unpleasant feeling abroad that the terrible form of an agent provocateur had overshadowed the misguided youth. But be that as it may, no one was ever more effectively 'hoist with his own petard'. When Bourdin was about fifty yards from the Observatory the bomb exploded, shattering his right hand to bits, and several pieces of iron penetrated his body. He staggered round and tried to walk down the hill, but sank to the ground after a few steps. He was picked up in a pitiable condition and died before he reached the hospital. So violent was the explosion that one of his fingers was found lying under the Observatory wall - so I have seen a bail fly off at cricket in the direction of long leg.[20]

That was one occasion when the British authorities did seem to suspect the handiwork of the Ochrana, but the reminiscences of Rudolf Rocker - the leader of the Jewish anarchists in London's East End - show that there were other occasions when violence of this mindless kind was narrowly averted through the vigilance of the *émigrés* themselves. Rocker comments that the London anarchists were haunted by the possibility that some of the refugees after 1905 might have become so embittered, so brutalized by the excesses of the white terror in their homelands, that they would undertake something desperate thereby endangering the survival of the anarchist movement and the future of the refugee community. Rocker's fears were realized when a young friend came to him in November 1909 and confided that a group of youthful exiles intended to bomb the forthcoming lord mayor's show. Rocker was aghast.

We discussed how to prevent the plan being carried out. He told me that the group was to meet the following evening at the home of one of its members in Whitehorse Lane in Stepney. I arranged with my friend Lazar Sabelinsky to go there with me, to talk to these young people. We found five of them there, including my informant, and one young girl. I told them we knew of their plan. I explained what a terrible blow it would be to all the people who had been able to find refuge in England. I asked them why they wanted to kill the Lord Mayor and innocent spectators. At first they denied the whole story. In the end they admitted it was true. I said that I was sure some Russian police agent had incited them to such a stupid and senseless outrage to discredit the whole revolutionary movement and to close England to all political refugees.

I don't know whether I convinced them by my arguments or whether it was only the fact that their plot had been discovered that decided them to drop it. There may have been a Russian police agent who had incited them for the reasons I feared. Or they may have been simply blind fanatics who had come from the unhealthy atmosphere of the conditions in Russia, where every policeman and every public dignitary, Governor or Mayor, was an instrument of despotism and oppression. Those conditions in Russia had given rise to such terrible things as the theory of unmotivated terror, directed against the entire bourgeoisie as a class, no matter whom it hit. [21]

Ochrana agents found fertile ground on which to work, and a community of *émigrés* in which to submerge. They engendered fear and distrust throughout the refugee community for no one could be certain that his neighbour or his best friend was not secretly working for the police. Nor was it just the agents of the Ochrana who infiltrated the movements of these exiled revolutionaries. In 1906 Rocker and the Jewish anarchists opened the Free Workingman's Club in Jubilee Street in the East End. This anarchist club quickly became the focus of much *émigré* activity because it offered a café, a library, and meeting-rooms. Any sympathetic political group could book the club's meeting-room for its own gatherings, and most of the refugee political organizations made use of these facilities. Naturally, for those who wished to monitor the activities of the dissident groups Jubilee Street was godsend. The anti-tsarist movement was so riddled with informers and agents from so many different police forces that one is tempted to regard it as a movement of *agents provocateurs* all inciting one another to commit outrages. A former anarchist commented in 1906 that an earlier club, the Club Autonomie, was closed simply because it had become a notorious rendezvous for spies in the pay of almost every European government who kept their masters well-informed on anarchist plans and activities in Britain. [22] Scotland Yard certainly had informants within the anarchist community, and Macnaghten boasted that his intelligence sources in anarchist circles were so good that he would have been notified within twenty-four hours of any projected plot hatched by refugee extremists. [23] He commented further that danger did not lie within the refugee organizations so much as with mentally unbalanced individuals who were almost impossible to stop. This was a comment made for the benefit of the public; Scotland Yard actually knew very little about what went on in the *émigré* community, thought this was probably due as much to language difficulties as to security precautions taken by the revolutionaries. There seems to be very little doubt that the refugee community was honeycombed with spies and informers. Genuine revolutionaries had to be very careful when they planned 'expropriations', and often their wives and mistresses were kept uninformed deliberately for their own protection and to lessen the risk of a careless word alerting some spy or agent in the wider society. England was showing increasing signs of intolerance towards aliens whom it had begun to regard as a serious threat both physically and culturally.

English reactions to outrages committed by refugees can be more easily understood within the wider context of British attitudes towards immigrants from the Baltic provinces or Jewish exiles escaping religious persecution. Even before the turn of the century it was possible to discern a growing animosity towards the increasing flood of aliens into England. Competition for jobs was thought to be an important element of this, although there is little evidence that *émigrés* did compete directly for scarce jobs outside the East End, and even there, as we have seen, they tended to favour old-fashioned handicrafts rather than competing for factory jobs with the English. Nevertheless, the fear of competition certainly existed and constituted an obvious cause of hostility towards immigrants amongst British workers.

There had already been two attempts made before 1900 to establish organizations to lobby for a restrictive policy. The first, the Society for the Suppression of the Immigration of Destitute Aliens, had been founded as early as 1886, and although its records have not survived, there are reports of occasional rowdy public meetings in the East End at which immigration was condemned roundly and resolutions passed demanding an immediate restriction policy. The government soon responded by the appointment of a Parliamentary Select Committee on Immigration which seemed to take the steam out of this particular organization and it quietly lapsed.[24]

The select committee failed to produce any government action on immigration, and consequently six years later a new pressure group was established named the Association for Preventing the Immigration of Destitute Aliens. By this time the situation of British working men had become desperate. Britain was gripped by the great depression of the 1890s at a time when events on the continent had increased immigration greatly. This new association failed for a similar reason to the earlier society, namely that both groups failed to appoint representatives from amongst the East End workers to their executive committees. The executives of both groups were top-heavy with politicians, peers and bourgeois businessmen. Decidedly not the sort of leadership to appeal to the labouring classes the East End in whose name the association claimed to act. These restrictionists from the middle and upper classes were motivated by ethnic or cultural prejudice and sought to use the economic fears of the East End workers as a convenient cloak to disguise a less rational alarm over the growing influx of East European aliens. The restrictionist movements not only neglected to recruit working men as members of their executives, but they also failed to include representatives from the trade unions or even leading East End employers. As a result, the associations were viewed with scepticism by most East Enders to a degree which led the founder of a later and more successful society to comment ruefully that it was one thing to want to help the working man, but it was another to get him to allow such help to be offered, let alone to accept it.

The London Working Man is not an easy master to serve. He is so accustomed to being bullied or flattered that he hardly feels quite at home when he is treated like a man. I cannot bully, nor can I flatter. Consequently, the working man is not quite sure whether he likes or dislikes me; whether he trusts or distrusts. Further, he has a lurking suspicion that he is a very much better man than I am, and knows much better than I do how things should be done. This makes it a difficult matter to consolidate him into one resolute whole, without which little can be accomplished.[25]

Although these early attempts at immigration restriction met with failure, a huge, untapped reservoir of illiberal sentiment directed against *émigrés* certainly existed. Such prejudices were mobilized effectively when in 1900 the Conservative member of the House of Commons for the Stepney division helped to found the British Brothers' League. Major William Eden Evans-Gordon was a former officer from the Indian Army, and he placed his formidable logistical talents at the disposal of the new society. Furthermore, he took care to include from the outset a number of resident East Enders in the organization's executive. Finally, unlike earlier leaders, his manifest and sincere interest in the welfare of his constituents made him a trusted and respected figure amongst native East Enders.

The British Brothers' League was not a propaganda organization, and it did not set out primarily to persuade people that the presence of large numbers of foreigners snatched the bread from the mouths of English workers. This it regarded as self-evident and eschewed public debate as a matter of policy, believing that the only result would be altercations and intransigence from both sides. It concentrated instead on preaching to the converted and sought to draw together all those East Enders who felt threatened by the alien influx and to turn them into a powerful pressure group in the hope of influencing parliament to enact restrictive legislation. The measure of its success can be seen in its membership, which eventually exceeded 45,000.[26]

The real strength of the British Brothers' League lay in its organization. It was a genuine East End, grass-roots association to which Evans-Gordon had grafted a quasi-military structure based upon a 'section' of 100 men. Ten of these local sections formed a 'ward', and each section elected its own delegate to the executive committee which decided the League's policy. Moreover, to ensure rank-and-file participation, each section delegate was instructed to form a subcommittee of four men from his section to discuss ways and means of implementing the general policies enunciated at executive level.

This was an impressive and viable structure and to it was added the all-important policy – for the impoverished East End – that membership was free. A man joined the League by enrolling and no dues were required. Naturally this was a two-edged sword. The high nominal membership ensured that as a pressure group the League commanded respectful attention, but its financial situation was precarious. Its officials were

required to work on a voluntary basis, and the League relied upon public
collections at its mass meetings and gifts from wealthy sympathizers to maintain its existence. In this its success was obvious, for there was no doubting the League's vitality. Its mass rallies were enormously popular, attracting thousands. Almost every member of parliament who represented an East End constituency found it wise to attend the League's public meetings, or at least to tender an apology for his absence, whilst aliens or members of the public who sympathized with the plight of the exiles were ejected from the meetings if they rose to protest.

The League spread to other areas of England outside London and meetings were held in support of its policies on immigration restriction in Leicester, Bedford and Kettering. It also spawned a parliamentary offshoot in 1903, known as the Immigration Reform Association, with a general committee of over 100 members including members of parliament from all parties, peers, clergymen and other public figures. It proposed to bring the 'real facts' of immigration to the attention of parliament and the general public, to provide experienced speakers on the subject, and to produce pamphlets in support of restrictive legislation. By 1905 the tide of unfavourable British reaction to Russian Jews and ethnic *émigrés* was flowing fast. It was unfortunate that the impetus for restriction coincided with the rapid increase in the number of refugees fleeing from the white terror in the Baltic provinces of the Russian empire.

In August 1903 the Royal Commission on Alien Immigration, which had been sitting since the previous year, gave the restrictionist movement a substantial boost by reporting unequivocally in favour of restriction. Although the commission found that the feared alien flood was a product of fevered imaginations, and that the total number of immigrants was small, it recommended the establishment of an Immigration Department whose officers would be empowered to investigate the circumstances, health and character of immigrants and to report dubious immigrants to a court of summary jurisdiction that could refuse them permission to land. Aliens who broke the law were to be deported, as were those with criminal records or even suspected criminals, prostitutes, pimps and persons of notorious character without visible means of support who were a charge on the public (except through ill health). Many other petty restrictions were recommended, and in general the Royal Commission satisfied the most vigorous proponents of restriction. Its recommendations amounted to a wholesale repudiation of Britain's traditional policies of asylum for refugees and refusal to make distinctions between rich and poor *émigrés*.[27]

Following an abortive attempt at legislation in 1904, Balfour's Conservative government finally enacted an Aliens Restriction Bill which received Royal assent in August 1905. The Act was far less rigorous than the recommendations of the Royal Commission, though any such Act seriously weakened the position of refugees in Britain. Under the terms of this Act an alien who had been excluded could appeal against the decision to an Immigration Board of three members, one of whom was a magistrate. Refugees from religious persecution were guaranteed right of entry into Britain. Similarly, alien criminals were to be deported if discovered, and they were not permitted to enter the country if they had been sentenced abroad for an extraditable, non-political crime. Permission to land in Britain was not to be withheld on the grounds of poverty, although the home secretary was empowered to order the expulsion of any alien without trial or appeal if he had received poor relief within a year of landing, or been found guilty of vagrancy, or found to be living in insanitary conditions due to overcrowding.

These exceptions were wide-ranging, and the Act proved to be ineffective and difficult to implement. Every refugee after the 1905 Revolution in Russia could claim fairly to be a religious or political exile, and the 'crimes' of the revolutionaries were easily shown to be politically motivated. When did an 'expropriation' become a plain robbery and cease to be a political crime? Was the murder of a Russian government official a political assassination or a criminal act? Such distinctions could not be drawn easily.

Not only was the Aliens Restriction Act almost impossible to enforce, but the Liberals, led by Sir Henry Campbell-Bannerman, in opposition had resisted it firmly, as had the Independent Labour Party. Obviously, the Act would be allowed to fall into desuetude when the Liberals were returned to office, even if the Conservatives had been able to design a set of workable regulations to accompany the Act. The regulations, however, made so many classes of immigrant immune from investigation that they effectively rendered the Act a piece of useless window-dressing. Nevertheless, it did represent the genuine concern of many Englishmen about the immigration of Jews and ethnic minorities from Russia. Towards the end of the nineteenth century, Queen Victoria had felt very strongly that political revolutionaries should be excluded from Britain, and she had written to the prime minister in 1894 expressing her concern that her government continued to allow 'these monstrous anarchists and assassins to live here and hatch their horrible plots in our country'.[28] These feelings were widespread, and the continuing occurrence of terrorist outrages and assassinations throughout Europe and America only served to reinforce them. Nevertheless, at the time of the Aliens Act, England had been spared the worst of these campaigns of revolutionary expropriation and violence. But the calm was soon to end; the next decade disabused many Englishmen of the notion that revolutionary violence was something that concerned excitable foreigners on the continent or in the United States. In 1914 Sir William Macnaghten encapsulated this view and demonstrated something of that infuriating mix of cultural chauvinism and xenophobia that was typical of many Ango-Saxons at this time.

I have always held the belief that anarchism has never tapped root in
this country. It is foreign to the nature of the British. Although we are
inundated with the scum of other countries, and various parts of
London swarm with Nihilists from Russia, Advanced Socialists from
Germany and Communists from France (to say nothing of a large
contingent of knifing Neapolitans), yet all these gentry are perfectly
well aware that, if they begin throwing bombs about in the London
streets, the British workman (honest fellow though occasional grum-
bler that he is!) would be the first person to hoof them out of the
country with an uncompromising and hobnailed boot, and that then
the gates of their very last city of refuge would be banged, bolted, and
barred against them. It is this that has given, and that continues to give
to England a very great immunity from the crimes which so often
terrorize the dwellers on the Continent. A little frothy speech in our
London parks does very little harm as a rule and blows off an infinity of
steam. It is only when there is a probability that the said froth may
become flecked with blood that the authorities need adopt repressive
measures.[29]

Yet even as these words were published, the march of events had left
Macnaghten and those who thought like him far behind; by 1914 he was
an elderly anachronism. For between the enactment of the Aliens'
Restriction legislation and the outbreak of the First World War, an
outbreak of revolutionary violence and bloodshed in London's East End
removed once and for all the comforting prejudice that the English
enjoyed some form of divine dispensation, enabling them to avoid the
worst excesses of the wave of political violence then sweeping across the
world. The events in the East End were destined to have a major impact
not only in Britain but also 12,000 miles away in Australia.

FOOTNOTES

1   William J. Fishman, *East End Jewish Radicals 1875-1914*, London, 1975,
    p. 4.
2   ibid., p. 6.
3   ibid., p. 22.
4   Only two and a half million remained a decade later to become citizens of
    Soviet Russia. A similar number had been surrendered to the reconstituted
    nation of Poland and the other successor states of Eastern Europe, while a
    further 500,000 emigrated. Probably 330,000 died either in the armies or
    as victims of the civil war, or through pogroms and starvation. See 'The
    Jews in Russia', *Observer Review*, 23 February 1969.

5 Michael Futrell, *Northern Underground: Episodes of Russian Revolutionary Transport and Communications Through Scandinavia and Finland*, London, 1963, p. 25. Karl Marx himself took advantage of British sanctuary after being expelled from Paris in 1849 and remained until his death thirty-four years later.

6 Bernard Gainer, *The Alien Invasion: The Origins of the Aliens Act of 1905*, London, 1972, pp. 2-3.

7 ibid., p. 3.

8 Christine Bolt, *Victorian Attitudes to Race*, London, 1971, p. 214.

9 George R. Sims (ed.), *Living London: Its Work and Its Play, Its Humour and Its Pathos, Its Sights and Its Scenes*, London, 1906, 3 vols, vol. 1, p. 27.

10 Donald Rumbelow, *The Houndsditch Murders and the Siege of Sidney Street*, London, 1973, pp. 132-3.

11 Ronald Seth, *The Russian Terrorists; The Story of the Narodniki*, London, 1866, p. 270.

12 Jacob Katz, *Jews and Freemasons in Europe 1723-1939*, Cambridge, USA, 1970, pp. 171-3.

13 After 1905 many revolutionaries languished in tsarist prisons. The revolutionary terrorists paid particular attention to their treatment and welfare. Warders and prison officials who were known to treat such prisoners brutally were tracked down and killed in reprisal. Ronald Seth, op. cit., p. 281.

14 Water Kendall, *The Revolutionary Movement in Britain 1900-21; The Origins of British Communism*, London, 1969, p. 80.

15 The full story of this voyage can be found in Michael Futrell, op. cit., p. 69 passim.

16 *Hansard Paliamentary Debates*, 4th series, vol. 22, col. 83.

17 Ronald Hingley, *The Russian Secret Police: Muscovite, Imperial Russian and Soviet Political Security Operations 1565-1970*, London, 1970, p. 90 passim.

18 ibid., pp. 80-1.

19 Victor Serge, *Memoirs of a Revolutionary 1901-1941*, Oxford, 1963 pp. 19-20.

20 Melville Macnaghten, *Days of My Years*, London, 1914, pp. 79-80.

21 Rudolf Rocker, *The London Years*, London, 1956, p. 192.

22 W.C. Hart, *Confessions of an Anarchist*, London, 1906, p. 18.

23 Melville Macnaghten, op. cit., p. 83.

24 Bernard Gainer, op. cit. pp. 60-1.

25 ibid., pp. 62-3.

26 ibid., p. 63.

27 Royal Commission on Alien Immigration, 1903. Report, cf. 1741, passim.

28 G.E. Buckle (ed.), *The Letters of Queen Victoria*, 3rd series, 3 vols, London, 1932, vol. 2, p. 414.

29 Melville Macnaghten, op. cit., pp. 78-9.

2
THE
TERROR
IN
LONDON

Among the many *émigrés* who fled to England from Russia after 1905 were some who were destined to achieve notoriety for a brief period early in 1911. The majority of political refugees made careful distinctions between countries and governments and viewed England as a haven that was not to be disturbed by resort to criminal activities. But these young activitists rejected this view as cowardly and self-deceptive, despising all existing administrations as corrupt capitalistic facades that masked the exploitation of the lower orders by a spurious claim to a democratic electoral system. The British government was regarded as no better than repressive continental governments, and the experiences of these *émigrés* with the Russian police and tsarist bureaucracy had given rise to a hatred of all police and government officials as representatives of vicious and brutalized power structures. Such attitudes burst upon the unsuspecting British public with a violence that removed for all time the agreeable British belief that England was protected from the terrorism then over-running Europe. It is to the credit of British politicians and administrators that they did not permit the events of 1911 to induce the shameful panic that its mere threat was to occasion in Western Australia towards the end of the same year.

At the beginning of 1909, however, all this was merely foreshadowed when several of the young Lettish refugees from Russia's Baltic provinces met and formalized their relationship in the 'Leesma' (Flame) group as part of a loose international structure of anti-tsarist anarchists. Accounts vary regarding the numerical strength of the Leesma cell. Scotland Yard's Special Branch thought it was a comparatively small group of Lettish immigrants who were really criminals and who used the cover of politics to disguise the motives for their burglaries and expropriations.[1] This presumption became the official orthodoxy of the City of London police force in its dealings with the press after members of the Leesma organization had become wanted men. The police persistently refused to accept the political motivation that underlay Leesma crimes despite the evidence to demonstrate its existence. In this the police might well have been motivated by the deportation provisions in the 1905 Aliens Act. Under this Act, an immigrant could be deported if convicted of a criminal offence, but not if the offence was a political crime. It was in the interests of the police, therefore, that such activities should be regarded as criminal and not political. Hence the statement from Special Branch: 'They appear to have formed part of a section of foreign criminals who used the term "Anarchy" to cover their otherwise nefarious callings. Their real object, it would appear, was not the furtherance of an anarchical movement or conspiracy, but plunder and robbery for personal gain.'[2]

Other opinions of the Leesma organization, however, assessed it as significantly more extensive than had Special Branch. The immigrant newspaper *Rankpelnis*, which helped to keep the different groups of antitsarists in touch with one another, disclosed that there were twenty-eight members of the Leesma group, whilst the police informant who later betrayed two of the men to the authorities had said that the group numbered about fifteen.[3] Both views were not mutually exclusive; it seems likely that this smaller group was only a cell in a larger organization. *Rankpelnis* stated that this group, number 5, was involved in the Houdsditch murders and the Sidney Street siege, but that all twenty-eight members of the London organization had gone into hiding by the end of 1910.[4]

The members of group 5 were a strange assortment. Jacob Fogel appears to have been the original leader. After the collapse of the 1905 Revolution, the sixteen-year-old Fogel had fled from Russia where the authorities accused him of participating in the murders of five men. He became an expropriator and was reputed to be a very dangerous person. The Special Branch kept him under surveillance in London. Fogel had a friend nicknamed 'Bifsteks', who introduced his landlord, Charles Perelman, to Fogel in 1908. Perelman was a fellow refugee and many of the group stayed with him for short periods during 1909. Fogel and 'Bifsteks' shared one of Perelman's rooms. A third lodger with whom these two were friendly was William Sokolow, known to everyone as Joseph. He also came from Russia and was a watchmaker by trade, which provided him with the opportunity for reconnoitring prospective targets for possible expropriations by the group. After an attempted holdup in the suburb of Tottenham in 1909, Perelman ordered both Fogel and 'Bifsteks' to leave his house; he wanted no unpleasantness with the police of his new country. But before Fogel and 'Bifsteks' left they shared their room for one night with a fellow Lettish refugee named Fritz Svaars. Fritz was a locksmith and had returned recently from America where a reward of $2000 was being offered for him for a number of expropriations. He was also wanted by the tsarist police in Riga for robbery and the murder of a policeman. Upon the departure of Fogel and 'Bifsteks', Perelman took in another new lodger named George Gardstein, who was wanted by the German police for expropriations, and when Jacob Fogel eventually withdrew from active participation, it was

the dynamic Gardstein who succeeded to the leadership of the Leesma
group.
In addition to the lodgers, Charles Perelman's house also became a
regular meeting-place for other recruits to the group. Yourka Dubof,
John Rosen and Karl Hoffman all associated with Svaars and Gardstein
in the three months that they were Perelman's tenants. Dubof and Rosen
were Letts who apparently had no criminal records in Russia, but Karl
Hoffman was a killer. Hoffman's real name was Trautman, and information later supplied to the City of London police from Riga indicated that
he was wanted for complicity in no less than sixteen murders. He was
an expropriator of the most dangerous kind.[5] Another occasional caller
was Jacob Peters, also from Riga and an active member of the Lettish
Social Democratic Party. Peters was Fritz Svaars's cousin, and the two
had once shared a common political viewpoint. Fritz's friendship with
George Gardstein, however, had led to an apparent alteration in his
outlook, and Peters found that the erstwhile Social Democrat had begun
to espouse the views of an anarchist. This occasioned a political quarrel
and Peters moved to lodgings of his own. Finally, the back room of
Charles Perelman's house was rented by a young Russian girl named
Nina Vassileva. Vassileva and George Gardstein soon became lovers, and
Nina moved like a moth around the edge of the Leesma flame. Nina
Vassileva performed one other important social function for group
members in that - according to the recollections of Charles Perelman's
son - she provided some form of collective masturbation or relief
massage to ease the sexual tensions of these young and healthy men who
subjected themselves to security-based restrictions concerning the level of
intimacy they could enjoy with women.
These individuals comprised the central core of group 5, and Fogel's
role seems to have been more that of co-ordinator of the wider organization than direct participator in group 5's expropriations. It appears that
these Lettish groups were organized on a system analogous to the 'circle'
method of the Irish Fenian Brotherhood. Under this plan, no member,
save perhaps the co-ordinator, knew the names of more than a small
selection of his comrades. Thus, if a cell was infiltrated by an Ochrana
spy, or if one of the comrades turned traitor, he could only destroy his
own group and not the entire organization. This *modus operandi* was
adopted by the Leesma people to reduce the risks from traitors to a
minimum. Group 5 was still recruiting when Fogel himself almost came
to grief through his involvement in a Leesma expropriation which
became popularly known as the Tottenham Outrage. The close call and
the consciousness of police surveillance made Fogel a very cautious and
circumspect man after this time. (Group 5 does not appear to have participated in this operation and did not come fully up to strength until the
following year.)
On Saturday 23 January 1909 about mid-morning, two young Letts
named Jacob Lepidus and Paul 'elephant' Hefeld loitered in the street at

the front gates of Schnurmann's rubber factory in Chestnut Road, Tottenham. They both carried automatic pistols, and they were waiting for the arrival of the wages clerk with the pay-roll for the factory workers. The pay-roll was later estimated to be about £80. Shortly after 10.30 a.m. the factory car drew up at the front gates and the wages clerk alighted, carrying the money in a canvas bag. As he walked between Lepidus and Hefeld to the factory, he was attacked and thrown to the ground. The car driver, Joseph Wilson, braked and flung himself on Lepidus in an attempt to help the struggling wages clerk. Jacob Lepidus proved to be a proficient and experienced street-fighter, and to his surprise the driver quickly found himself thrown over Jacob's head, landing on his back on the roadway. At this stage the bulky Hefeld took a hand and, drawing his pistol, opened fire on the prone and winded driver, who rolled himself desperately across the road under this barrage of shots and miraculously missed being killed or even seriously wounded, though his leather overcoat and his clothes were cut to pieces by the hail of bullets.

Hefeld and Lepidus then grabbed the wages bag and ran. From the police-station directly opposite, a small party of officers and men, hearing the sound of gunfire, had come rushing to investigate. The leading figures in the chase were armed only with their wooden truncheons, which were of little use against the automatic pistols of the robbers. There followed a chase that was Keystonian in duration and circumstances, but with an element of tragi-comedy.

The two fugitives first ran off on foot, hotly pursued by several of the local constables furiously pedalling their bicycles and waving their truncheons. Others, who had joined the chase even earlier, were afoot, and two of them, Constables Tyler and Newman often closed to within 9 yards of their quarry before being forced behind cover by a fusillade. The driver, Wilson, recovering his aplomb, drove up in the factory car, and Newman climbed into it while Tyler ran alongside with the factory manager. At this stage, when one of the Letts stopped to reload his pistol, Newman - assuming the advantage now lay with the pursuers - instructed Wilson to try to run the men down. Nothing loathe, Wilson accelerated the car towards the men who, instead of panicking and running away, calmly crouched in the roadway and simultaneously opened fire on the approaching vehicle. Newman was shot through the cheek, Wilson suffered a flesh wound in the neck, the car was put out of commission with a smashed windscreen and radiator and, tragically, a small ten-year-old boy was killed by a shot through the body as he ran for cover.

The gunmen ran on towards the marshes whilst the police followed at a more discreet distance, now armed with firearms from the station's armoury. With pistols in their pockets the police leapt on their bicycles and resumed the chase. One of the cyclists was armed with a cutlass which he waved aloft as he pedalled along. Constable Tyler again drew close to the fugitives, whereupon Hefeld turned and shot him through

the neck. He quickly lost consciousness and bled to death before medical
attention could be provided. Telephone messages were sent to nearby police - stations, and policemen were instructed to converge on the Tottenham marshes. Some of these new pursuers were armed, but the bulk of them were equipped only with their truncheons.

Hefeld and Lepidus had by now reached the marshes, and the chase traversed the uneven ground of the wasteland. They came eventually to Tottenham mill-stream, where they found the bridge blocked by labourers who had been working on the other side of the stream. As the workmen ran towards the bridge, the gunmen opened fire on them, wounding several. The remainder rapidly evacuated the bridge and took cover wherever they could. Having gained the bridge the two men rested and regained their breath while keeping their pursuers at bay with pistol shots whenever they came too close. Another policeman was wounded at this stage.

Having rested a little, the two men ran on, conserving their energies by spells of jogging followed by periods of walking. By this time Hefeld had taken over most of the shooting, with Lepidus acting as gunbearer and loader of the automatic not in use. Eventually they reached the other side of the marsh to find themselves on a road down which ran a tram line. They sprinted after a passing tram and commandeered it. The driver escaped and hid on the tram's roof, but the two desperate men forced the conductor to drive the tram for them. The police in their turn took possession of another tram and continued their pursuit. They also commandeered a horse-drawn advertising cart, and this was gaining quickly on the fugitives when Hefeld coolly disposed of the horse with a single, well-aimed shot.

On the first tram an old man - a captive passenger - made a gesture which Jacob interpreted as an attempt to snatch his pistol. He spun round and shot the man through the throat. As the old fellow collapsed, Lepidus and Hefeld leapt off the tram and ran towards a horse-drawn milk-cart standing by the kerb. The milkman was gunned down and they drove off on his cart, lashing the horse with a whip. They soon wrecked the milk-cart and replaced it with a greengrocer's van, which was similarly appropriated. Lepidus drove whilst Hefeld sat at the tailboard and kept the pursuing police at bay with the pistols. The horse quickly became exhausted - Jacob had not realized that the brake was on - and the two men were forced to abandon this vehicle and take to their heels once more with a growing crowd of police closing in behind them. Eventually the robbers ran into a blind alley with a 6-foot fence at the end. Jacob clambered over, but the thick-set Hefeld fell back and, calling on his friend to save himself, put his pistol to his right temple and pulled the trigger. The bullet passed through Hefeld's head before exploding out his forehead on the other side, but it did not kill him. Before he could fire again, the police pounced on him and after a violent struggle he was captured and taken off to hospital for treatment. Meanwhile, Lepidus had taken refuge in a small cottage to which the police laid siege. Finally, cornered and with only two bullets left, he also turned his pistol on himself to better effect than his hapless compatriot. In hospital Hefeld refused to talk and died two weeks later of meningitis. The pay-roll was never recovered, and Scotland Yard were convinced that at some stage the two men had passed the bag to an accomplice, probably Jacob Fogel, and preferred to kill themselves rather than face interrogation, which might lead to the disclosure of their organization and accomplices to the police.

Both men had been members of the Lettish Social Democratic Party, and the Party vigorously repudiated any suggestion that Lepidus and Hefeld were officially sponsored expropriators, pointing out that the Social Democratic Party specifically forbade expropriation as a means of fund raising. Hefeld's room was so full of revolutionary literature that the authorities had to use a special car to carry it all away. Obviously, the men, who were sailors as well as expropriators, were also couriers in the England-based underground operation through which revolutionary propaganda was smuggled into the restive provinces of the tsarist empire.

The reaction of the London press to the deaths of Constable Tyler and the young boy was immediate and hostile. *The Times* headed its account of these events 'Shooting Outrage - Alien Robbers Run Amok - Three Deaths: Many Injured'. The story concentrated heavily on the fact that Hefeld and Lepidus had been immigrants.

The outrages were the work of men whose identity was yesterday thoroughly established as being members of the Russian revolutionary party, whose headquarters are known to be in London . . . One of the miscreants was known to the foreign service branch of the Metropolitan Police as Jacob. He is dead, having been shot through the head by a police-constable. (This was a common assumption until the Coroner's report showed that Jacob had shot himself.) The other is Paul Hefeld, about 25 years of age, who is now in the hospital suffering from a bullet wound in the head. Both these men come from the Baltic port of Riga, and have, it is believed, been engaged in conveying revolutionary literature, which is printed in the country, to Russia. For this purpose they posed as seamen, and when going on voyages to Russia could smuggle the papers about their persons and thus elude the officials both here and at the Russian ports.[6]

Nor was such animosity restricted only to the popular press. In the House of Commons, the government faced a censure motion for virtually suspending the operation of those parts of the Aliens Restriction Act relating to the power to refuse entry to undesirable aliens. Opposition speakers referred favourably to the restrictive legislation passed by Australia and the United States and suggested that Britain could gain from the experiences of these two nations. Here also, the speakers stressed the fact that the two Letts were immigrants.

Mr Claude Hay asked the Secretary of State for the Home Department whether he has taken steps to ascertain the antecedents of the alien murderers Jacob and Hefeld, both as regards the conditions under which they came to this country and the circumstances under which they lived in this country; whether Jacob or Hefeld, or both, were known to the police as being associated with revolutionaries or anarchists; and whether one or both of them were known to have been in possession of bombs since their arrival in this country? Mr Gladstone: All possible steps have been taken to trace the antecedents of these men. Hefeld is known to the Police as having been a seafaring man, and Jacob they believe was of the same occupation. Both had endeavoured to earn a living by work in this country. Both associated with certain Lettish countrymen of their own, known to be adherents of the Revolutionary party in Russia. The Police have no knowledge, and have not even heard it reported that either or both had been in possession of bombs.[7]

The government successfully weathered the storm, and the issue of alien immigration again faded into the background. The Tottenham incident, however, was only the prelude.

Although not directly involved in the Tottenham Affair, the members of group 5 had not been idle, and changes in habitat and additions to membership occurred that were to prove significant. Charles Perelman moved house and took the opportunity to rid himself of his lodgers. Fogel and 'Bifsteks' were ordered to leave shortly after the Tottenham crime, and Fritz Svaars, George Gardstein, Sokolow, and Nina Vassileva all found new lodgings in the East End as Perelman used one excuse after another to turn them out. Although Vassileva and Gardstein were lovers, they never shared accommodation. George Gardstein found himself a room at 44 Gold Street, which he rented under the name of Morin, one of his many aliases. He allowed his new landlord to believe he was a chemist because of the amount of laboratory equipment and chemicals he kept in his room. Occasionally, he disappeared for weeks at a time before reappearing and paying all the back rent. Presumably these absences coincided with expropriations or political missions back in Russia.

Fritz Svaars returned to Russia after the Tottenham robbery, and in January 1910 he was captured in Riga by the Russian secret police. He managed to keep his identity secret, although he endured a series of ferocious beatings, during which he was interrogated and under which he broke down. He was released on bail and shadowed wherever he went. Fritz wrote all this to his sister after he had given his shadows the slip and escaped abroad once more. He told her his head had felt soft due to the repeated bashings he received while in the Ochrana cells in Riga.[8] He returned to London with the intention of obtaining sufficient money for his wife and himself to emigrate to Australia, a preference that might be explained by the $2,000 reward on his head which precluded a return to the United States.

Like the other members of his group, Fritz frequented the anarchist club in Jubilee Street. It was an easy place to meet one's fellow countrymen in the anonymity of a crowd. Even Lenin found the Jubilee Street Club to his liking during his time in London.[9] Whilst there, Fritz made the acquaintance of a young Jewish girl named Luba Milstein. She was eighteen years old, and Fritz soon installed her in his lodgings as his mistress. Luba knew Fritz was married and intended to leave England for Australia with his wife, but she was besotted with him. She commented later, in a letter to her sister, that if Fritz had told her that it was midnight at midday she would have believed him. To Luba's dismay, however, she quickly found that not only did she have to share Fritz with his wife in Russia and with the rest of the Leesma group - from whose meetings she was always excluded - but she also had to share him with a strange friend from whom he apparently could not bear to be parted. It is in this way that Peter Piaktow, known as Peter the Painter, enters the story.

Peter the Painter was, and remains, an enigma. His early history is shrouded in myth, and little can be said with certainty other than that he too was a Lett, and that his name probably was not Piaktow. At a later date, the tsarist authorities identified him as a peasant from the Province of Courland, district of Goldingen, named Evan Evanovitch (Janis Janisoff) Jakle, alias Jaklis, who was wanted by the police at Goldingen for having absconded and evaded military service.[10] This was a very tentative identification and carried little conviction, although some corroborative evidence did emerge later in 1911. The commissioner of police for Marseilles was able to provide more information. According to the records of the French police, Piaktow arrived in Marseilles in 1908 and found work as a painter of street doors and house numbers. He turned up on several occasions when French police searched the known haunts of anarchists and revolutionaries, but apparently kept out of trouble. He had a reputation for violence and often disappeared with Russian friends for short periods. One of the firms he worked for, however, could not be traced by the police who had to rely on an account given by one of his French acquaintances. According to this informant, Peter Piaktow was the nephew of a colonel in the Russian army, a convinced socialist, and had been born in the Province of Courland. The name he used did not seem appropriate to his place of birth, as names from that part of the Baltic region did not usually terminate with 'ow', 'off', 'eff' or 'ski', but 'tis', 'tus' or 'vitsch'. 'Piaktow' was probably an alias. Additional information carefully gathered by the English police showed that Peter had been jailed for crimes committed during the 1905 Revolution. He arrived in Marseilles from Oran shortly after the assassination of the king of Portugal, and he professed to be familiar with nearly all the countries of western Europe. On the surface, he appears to have been a typically itinerant young Baltic *émigré* with revolutionary tendencies. The ghettoes and refugee areas of half of Europe were filled with similar people.

When he arrived in England, he moved in with Fritz Svaars and Luba Milstein. The room they shared was at 35 Newcastle Place, but this proved to be far too small to accommodate them. Not surprisingly, Luba resented the presence of this friend, and after five weeks they all moved to 59 Grove Street, where Fritz rented two rooms for them. The large front room was taken over by Peter, the smaller back room was used by Fritz and Luba. Fritz paid for both rooms, and Luba later commented that Fritz and Peter did not want to be separated. George Gardstein helped the three of them bundle their possessions onto a costermonger's barrow and move into their new premises.

Peter's front room seemed to become the headquarters for Leesma group 5, and Gardstein, Sokolow, Karl Hoffman, John Rosen, a barber, and Max Smoller, a sneak thief, became constant visitors.[11] Neither Fritz nor Peter had regular employment, and when Luba Milstein asked Fritz what his business was, she was curtly told to mind her own. The men carried pistols concealed in special pockets in their clothes. The group's meetings were conducted in Lettish to keep Luba and her friend Sara Trassjonsky - a regular visitor - from understanding what was going on.

Correspondence later found by the police in the room indicates that Leesma group number 5 was an odd collection of activists who apparently agreed to work together despite their political differences. It may be that their shared Lettish nationality over-rode lesser considerations of political ideology, or it may be a tribute to the persuasive powers of Peter Piaktow, but the group eventually included Social Democrats, anarchists and Socialist Revolutionaries, all co-operating in expropriation activities. The Tottenham robbery had already shown that Lettish Social Democrats would involve themselves in expropriations if they thought the chances of success were high enough to make the risks worth taking, and it seems probable that political labels were a minor consideration when the overall campaign against the hated regime of the tsar was taken into account.

If Peter the Painter provided the philosophical common ground for members of these different organizations to merge for a common purpose, it was George Gardstein who provided the dynamic leadership in the field that was necessary if successful expropriations were to be carried out. Gardstein was a man of action, a physically powerful and attractive individual with a forceful personality. Once a plan of action had been devised, Gardstein was the perfect lieutenant to put it into effect. Time was to show, however, that when he had to think quickly and act on his own initiative, George Gardstein became a man of irresolution, plagued by doubts.

Responsibility for the selection of Harris's jewellery shop as the group's next target is difficult to apportion. The shop was a new one, recently opened in the sleazy East End district of Houndsditch. It seems likely that the watchmaker Sokolow provided the information. The rear of the shop shared a common wall with the back fences of a row of tenement houses facing a cul-de-sac. Early in December 1910 two of these houses were rented by Max Smoller and Fritz Svaars. The third house in the group, which was known as Exchange Buildings, was used by the landlords to store goods and was empty at the time of the attempted robbery. Most of the neighbours assumed that the new tenants were newly weds who wanted privacy. The shutters often stayed up all day, and sometimes Nina Vassileva could be seen taking them down or walking out with a shawl over her face. Max and Sokolow stayed with Nina in the house and slept on furniture borrowed from Fritz's rooms and from George Gardstein.

Gardstein organized the details. He obtained several books on metals, with information about dissolving metal with corrosive chemicals and acid. He also procured a special metal-cutting tool with which to break open the jeweller's safe once it had been softened by chemicals and heat. From a well-known Italian anarchist, Enrico Mallatesta, he purchased a large cylinder of oxygen and a long length of rubber tubing, the intention being to use a mixture of oxygen and domestic gas to make a primitive but effective cutting torch. The back of the safe would be treated with acid and chemicals, then subjected to intense heat, and finally the metal cutters would be used to tear a hole in the weakened metal.

On the afternoon of 16 December, Leesma group 5 assembled for a final briefing in Peter Piaktow's room at 59 Grove Street. Nina was absent, being already in the house at number 11 Exchange Buildings, and Jacob Peters had arranged to go directly to the house that evening. The plan was simple. The would-be expropriators were to climb over the side fences of the two houses they had rented on each side of the empty house used for storage. There they would break through the brick wall at the rear of the yard, and then through the back wall of Harris's jewellery store. This part of the plan required finesse because Harris's safe stood in the back office of the jeweller's establishment against the rear wall. It was in full view of the front window to the street, and a light was left burning all night in the office so that policemen patrolling that beat could see at a glance whether any attempts were being made to interfere with it. The Leesma plan was to break through the wall directly behind the safe and cut it open from the rear. If the walls were breached carefully, and above all accurately, the robbery could proceed unobserved from the street window and would remain undiscovered until the safe was opened on Monday.

Because it was expected to be a lengthy and time-consuming affair, probably taking the entire weekend, the group divided into two shifts. The first consisted of Gardstein, Jacob Peters, Yourka Dubof, another member of the group, who came from Riga, and Max Smoller. The second shift included Fritz Svaars, Sokolow, Karl Hoffman, and another Lettish Social Democrat named Osip Federoff. John Rosen, the barber, was on standby in case anyone got sick. Peter the Painter seems to have held himself aloof from the practical side of the operation, apparently preferring to plan and co-ordinate the scheme. His room certainly became the headquarters for this ambitious operation and for all the meetings and activities of the group, and police records show that he participated in the general briefing session during the afternoon of Friday 16 December 1910.

The initial break-in could not begin until after 7 in the evening on Friday when Millard Brothers, the owners, took the last of their stored Christmas stock from 10 Exchange Buildings and locked the door. When the coast was clear, the first shift of expropriators clambered over the fence into the empty yard and began attacking the rear wall of the outside toilet. They used drills and chisels, and the noise in the quiet of a winter's evening must have been very loud. Yourka Dubof went outside and wandered about the nearby streets to ascertain whether the noise could be heard easily, and to gauge any public reactions to it. It was the eve of the Jewish sabbath, however, and the streets were deserted. Moreover, it was developing into a wild and windy night at a time of the year when it was too cold to be out for pleasure. Everything seemed to be going according to plan.

The quietness of the streets had been deceptive. The noise of the scraping and drilling had been heard and had caused concern amongst the neighbours. The residents next-door to Harris's shop had become sufficiently alarmed by 10 pm by what sounded suspiciously like a break-in attempt, to send Max Weil, the man of the house, to search for a constable to whom he could report the unsettling noises. He quickly found a young constable named William Piper on patrol and brought him back to hear the strange sounds. They listened together, and Piper was forced to agree that it did sound as though someone was attempting to break through the brickwork at the rear of the jeweller's shop. Piper, in order to ensure that there was no innocent explanation, walked around the corner into the cul-de-sac in which Exchange Buildings were situated. He knocked on the door of number 11 and was immediately struck by the air of furtive reticence about the man who opened the door. Instead of asking whether some sort of construction work was underway at the back of the house, Piper – convinced that a robbery was afoot – blurted out the bizarre inquiry, 'Is the missus in?' Gardstein, probably nonplussed to be asked that particular question in the circumstances, muttered that his missus had gone out. Piper replied, 'Right, I will call back,' and left quickly. He had not gone far before meeting two constables, named Walter Choat and Ernest Woodhams, from adjoining beats. He told them of his suspicions and requested Woodhams to stand at the entrance to the cul-de-sac and Choat to watch the jewellery store in Houndsditch whilst he ran to fetch assistance. He neglected to inform Choat and Woodhams that he had observed a man watching him from the shadows at the entrance to the cul-de-sac who had walked quickly away when Piper approached him, and he also neglected to tell them that he had already called at number 11 Exchange Buildings, thereby tipping off the criminals that they had come to the attention of the police. So the scene was set for disaster, with the expropriators forewarned of police interest in them and trapped in a dead-end street with its only exit covered by the watching Constable Woodhams.

Piper soon returned with reinforcements. He brought Sergeants Bentley, Bryant and Tucker, and Constables Martin, Strongman and Smoothey. Max Weil took Bentley into his house to hear the noises, but as they were talking, the hammering stopped. Perhaps the working men had heard their conversation, or perhaps they had just received Gardstein's warning that police were in the vicinity. Because Piper was only a probationary constable, he was instructed to change places with Choat and continue the watch on the front of Harris's shop. Smoothey was stationed on a nearby corner, and Woodhams remained at the entrance to the cul-de-sac. Bentley then led the others to the doorway of number 11 Exchange Buildings. Gardstein opened the door on Bentley's knock. 'Have you been working or knocking about inside?' No answer. Bentley then asked whether he had anybody in the house who could understand English, and if he did to fetch them down. Gardstein left the door pushed to and walked halfway up the nearby stairs. No one came. Bentley pushed the door open and stepped into the entrance hall. Gardstein's legs were visible on the stairs, but his face was in darkness. The other policemen crowded forward.

'Is anybody working here?'
'No!'
'Anybody in the back?'
'No!'
'Can I have a look in the back?'
'Yes.'
'Show us the way.'

'In there,' said Gardstein, pointing into the room. Bentley stepped further inside, and as he did the back door was flung open and a gunman (Jacob Peters) walked rapidly into the room firing a pistol.[12] Gardstein, on the stairs, also opened fire on the unarmed police, and in the crossfire Bentley went down with several wounds, one of which severed his spinal cord. Bryant, who had been behind him, staggered into the street with bullets in the arm and chest. Woodhams ran to help and received a shot in the leg which shattered his thigh bone. Strongman and Tucker then found themselves in the firing line. Tucker reeled back, hit by two shots, one in the hip and the other in the heart. Strongman assisted Tucker to the end of the cul-de-sac before he collapsed and died on the roadway. Constable Martin ran for cover and took shelter in a house across the road. He did nothing to help his comrades and afterwards, to protect his reputation, he lied about the events.[13]

The gang now burst from the house and raced for the exit from the cul-de-sac, blazing away with their automatic pistols at anything that moved. Constable Choat bravely tackled Gardstein and fought for his automatic mauser. Gardstein pulled the trigger, and Choat took four bullets in the left leg as he desperately wrestled the gun away from his body. Jacob Peters ran behind Choat and shot him twice in the back. As the dying constable fell to the ground he pulled Gardstein with him, and Max Smoller accidently shot his leader in the back as he tried to shoot the policeman. Finally, Choat was kicked repeatedly in the face to make him release his tenacious hold on the wounded Gardstein, who was then seized by two of the men later identified as Jacob Peters and Yourka Dubof, and half-dragged half-carried away. Nina Vassileva accompanied her lover and his comrades, and Max Smoller brought up the rear. Somehow they managed to assist the badly wounded Gardstein back to Peter the Painter's room at 59 Grove Street. They bundled Gardstein quickly up the stairs and laid him on Peter Piaktow's bed in the front room.

Back at the scene of the shootings, Sergeant Tucker was already dead. Sergeants Bentley and Bryant and Constables Choat and Woodhams were conveyed to nearby hospitals, but Bentley and Choat soon succumbed to their wounds. The expropriators' 'score' was three policemen dead and two wounded. This slaughter of unarmed officers was to incite the British public to a furious call for revenge, the vehemence of which caused a frightened émigré community to close ranks in expectation of a pogrom, thereby making the task of police attempting to track down and arrest the criminals very difficult.

In some ways, responsibility for the shootings could be laid at Constable Piper's door, in that he failed to inform anybody that the gang was aware of a likely police intervention. It is only fair to add, however, that Piper was a raw recruit who could quite easily have failed to perceive the relevance of this information. Moreover, the city police were never armed for investigating breaking and entering cases, and it is hard to see how knowledge of Piper's early activities at Exchange Buildings could have lessened the death toll. Gardstein's behaviour is also interesting. He appeared to be nonplussed and flustered by Bentley's interrogation at the front door, and his withdrawal to a position half-way up the stairs seems to betoken the actions of a man who was faced with a situation with which he was unable to cope. It could also be argued that Gardstein actually lured the police into the room where they would be caught in an enfilading crossfire between the back door and the stairs. This possibility is not borne out, however, by the conversation between Bentley and Gardstein, where the latter's monosyllabic responses to Bentley provide no evidence of any consciousness that he held the advantage. Gardstein's qualities of leadership seem questionable, and in this crisis he appeared to be out of his depth.

At 59 Grove Street, Peter Piaktow and Fritz Svaars were waiting in the front room when the men carried Gardstein in and laid him on the bed. He had been shot near the left shoulder-blade, and the bullet had passed right through the chest and bulged just under the skin in front. He was conscious, but in great pain. Luba Milstein and her friend Sara Trassjonsky were summoned from the back room to assist with the wounded man. Sara made up a cold compress for the wound in Gardstein's back and pulled off his boots. Meanwhile, the other members of group 5 held a hurried consultation and decided that the alarm should be given and the entire Leesma organization should go to ground, especially the members of their own cell. Unable to move any further, Gardstein remained in Peter the Painter's bed, beneath the mattress of which Jacob Peters carefully concealed the pistol he had used to murder the three policemen. George Gardstein was being set up to become the scapegoat for the whole group. The men then scattered in all directions, each putting as much distance as possible between Grove Street and himself without leaving the familiar area of London's East End.

Luba Milstein was not the stuff of which heroines are made. She became quite hysterical at being left in the house with a dying man. Sara Trassjonsky gave her the key to her own room nearby in Settle Street, and Luba thankfully left the mortally wounded man to the care of her friend. Fritz had ordered the women to collect all incriminating and personal papers in the two rooms and burn them before they left. He had further instructed them that if Gardstein died whilst they were still there, they were to pour paraffin over him and the bed and burn the place down in order to confuse the police. He made no mention of what was to become of the other lodgers in the building, though presumably in such an extremity they were all expendable. Gardstein, however, was a healthy and strong young man. He lingered on.

Luba Milstein was in a state of great nervous excitement and before proceeding to Sara's room she stopped to see Karl Hoffman at 36 Lindley Street. To her surprise, she found Fritz, Peter and Sokolow with him. Fritz sent her back to Grove Street to collect photographs and papers, but she was in a fearful panic. She told Sara the police were coming and they should both leave immediately. Sara, to her credit, refused to leave the wounded man despite Luba's entreaties and Gardstein's insistence. She elected to stay on, and Luba scuttled off to her friend's room in Settle Street. By 3 am Gardstein's condition had deteriorated so badly that Sara went to Luba and asked whether she knew a doctor who might come. Luba remembered seeing a doctor's hoarding in Yiddish nearby, and the two women slipped through the early morning gloom to call on Dr John Scanlon. Neither of them spoke English - Yiddish was their native tongue - and Scanlon, a locum, spoke no Yiddish. They made themselves understood, however, in broken French, and Scanlon agreed to come. Luba's nerve once again was not equal to the task, and she slipped away to Settle Street while the more resolute Sara accompanied

Scanlon to the bedside of the sick man. Gardstein told the doctor a friend
had shot him by mistake, and he refused to go to hospital. Scanlon could only prepare him a narcotic to dull the pain. Sara travelled back to the surgery with him and waited while he made up the mixture with which she then returned to George Gardstein. Scanlon, for some inexplicable reason, did not inform the police of this transaction, although it must have been obvious that something extremely odd was afoot. He arranged instead to visit Gardstein later in the morning to see how he was getting along.

Sara administered a draught of the medicine to Gardstein and then hurried to Karl Hoffman's room to bring the others up to date with events. Fritz directed her to return and to collect clothing, the tickets he had purchased for his passage to Australia, and any papers and photographs she could find. Sara bustled back and forth between Settle Street and Grove Street on this task, but could not bring herself to abandon the slowly dying man. She persuaded Luba to go with her on the visit about 9.15 am when the two women discovered that George Gardstein had finally died.

Both women panicked and ran to 36 Lindley Street, only to find Karl Hoffman there alone. Peter, Fritz and William Sokolow had already gone to earth. Fritz and Sokolow found refuge with a woman of Sokolow's acquaintance named Betsy Gershon, at 100 Sidney Street, while Peter the Painter stayed briefly with his friend Pavell Molchanoff. Gershon and Molchanoff were probably members of the Leesma organization, though not of cell 5. Hoffman refused to divulge the men's whereabouts to the women, but while they were with him, Pavell called round. Luba begged Sara and Pavell to return once more to Grove Street and gather up the photographs and papers she had left behind. She herself had become too hysterical to accompany them and decided to await their return at Molchanoff's place. To her surprise when she arrived, she found herself confronted by a clean-shaven Peter the Painter. Peter was intent on escape. He borrowed a small sum of money from Luba and then apparently vanished. Nobody can be quite sure what happened to him after this (though in later chapters several different scenarios involving Peter Piaktow will be discussed, together with a probable explanation of his behaviour).

Meanwhile, Pavell and Sara had returned to the deserted headquarters in Grove Street, where the thoroughly alarmed landlord refused to allow Sara to leave. He had no intention of facing on his own the inevitable police investigation into the dead body on his premises, and he insisted that because Sara was a known confidant of his now vanished tenants, she should remain to give some explanation to the authorities. Sara spent her time gathering the photographs and papers and burning them in the grate. Pavell returned to his lodgings in time to see Peter depart and to tell both Luba and Peter the bad news. It is important to remember that at this time the police had not been informed of Gardstein's condition.

The landlord at Grove Street did nothing other than ensure Sara Trassjonsky did not leave, and Dr Scanlon did not trouble to alert them until quite late in the morning of Saturday 17 December. Thus the members of group 5 had time to hide themselves and to decide on a course of action.

Only those on the first shift of expropriators who were actually engaged in the shooting affray went to ground. The others, including Luba Milstein and Sara Trassjonsky, believed that as they had not been at the scene of the murders, they were therefore not responsible for what had happened. Luba, Fritz and Peter the Painter felt involved because Gardstein had been brought to their rooms to die, so they too sought sanctuary within the wider refugee community in the East End. What the other members of group 5, and indeed the entire Leesma organization, failed to understand, was that under English law they were all culpable as accessories to murder and conspiracy. This facet of English jurisprudence was distinctly outlined by the coroner at the inquest on Sergeant Bentley.

The evidence renders it not impossible that Bentley was exposed to a crossfire from both stairs and room. In any case this point, it is my duty to tell you, makes no difference in the eye of the law. Any person engaged in the conspiracy to steal Mr Harris's jewels becomes responsible for a murder committed in the course of their common purpose. An accessory before the act, even though he were a long distance away from the scene of the felony at the time of the attempted commission of the murder, would become responsible for that crime. To quote the words of a modern writer on the law of evidence, 'Persons who are guilty of illegally conspiring together or of committing jointly any criminal offence are deemed to be mutual agents or confederates for the purpose only of the execution of the joint purpose. Accordingly any act done by any one of them in the execution of the common purpose is deemed the act of the others also, and is consequently admissible as evidence against them [14]

It was the *émigrés'* inability to comprehend this law of evidence that was to render those eventually brought to trial so embittered with British justice. To the refugees, the question of being an accessory seemed like legalistic cheese-paring. You either killed a man or you did not. If you did not pull the trigger of the murder weapon or yourself handle the bludgeon or knife, then you were not guilty of murder. Thus, while certain members of group 5 most directly implicated in the Houndsditch proceedings did go into hiding, the rest of the Leesma organization submerged quietly into the East End community and went about their daily business, unaware of the danger of their situation. Moreover, George Gardstein's death cleared the way for him to be saddled with the entire blame for the fatalities. As it turned out, the authorities themselves seemed almost anxious that this account of events be accepted as orthodoxy.

And the police at long last were beginning to act. Scanlon finally discharged his duty and informed the authorities that a man with a gunshot wound was hiding at 59 Grove Street. After the events of the previous night, the police moved quickly, and a detective-constable named Leeson burst into the back room in time to catch Sara Trassjonsky in the act of burning photographs and papers in the grate. Leeson confiscated what remained, and Sara became the first person associated with the group to be taken into custody. Gardstein's body was quickly identified as that of the man who had opened the door to the police at 11 Exchange Buildings the previous night, and further rapid progress was made when Luba Milstein's brothers forced her to go to the police and give herself up. Descriptions of Fritz Svaars, William Sokolow, Yourka Dubof, Osip Federoff, Peter Piaktow, Jacob Peters, and Nina Vassileva were slowly assembled and circulated widely through the press. The descriptions were vague and very general, but with the help of *émigré* informants the police began to make progress and several arrests were made in the ensuing weeks. Peter, Fritz and Sokolow, however, remained at large.

The press, as might have been expected, indulged in an orgy of anti-alien sentiment. The murders seemed to reinforce all the prejudices against Russian and Baltic immigrants, and the East End population went in dread of the outbreak of a pogrom of revenge such as they had been accustomed to endure in Russia. The press, however, probably acted as a safety valve in this situation, and no organized persecution resulted. Moreover, the East End was flooded with plain-clothes detectives and policemen in disguise looking for clues, and the local inhabitants were probably protected as much as they were intimidated by these hundreds of police spies in their midst. Even *The Times* succumbed to the temptation to make anti-alien capital out of the Houndsditch crimes and to imply that something far stronger than the 1905 Aliens Restriction Act was needed if similar outrages were to be avoided in the future.

That fact - the unarmed condition of the police - will at once impress itself upon the public, excited, grieved and indignant as they are at such a murderous outrage committed in the heart of London. We do not know, unfortunately, who committed it, but there are many reasons for believing that they are aliens, and either Russians or Poles ... The whole affair has taken place in or near a neighbourhood which is given up to aliens ... and is the greatest receiving ground of the poorest class of aliens from Western Europe ... Nor is anything to be said against a large proportion of the population in the Whitechapel area. But it does harbour some of the worst alien anarchists and criminals who seek our too hospitable shore. And these are men who use the pistol and the knife. The present affair inevitably recalls the extraordinary and fatal outrage which occurred at

*Tottenham less than two years ago, when two of these alien criminals
planned to commit a robbery in the open street ... They just pulled
out revolvers and ran down the street firing at all and sundry. Now the
British criminal never does a thing like that. Burglars very rarely use
firearms at all, and a regular concerted attack on policemen who are
demanding admittance to a house in the performance of their duty is
almost unknown. There can be little or no doubt that the perpetrators
of the reckless crimes on Friday night are of the same class as those at
Tottenham in January of last year. In that case they used their
weapons not only in the most reckless manner, but with extraordinary
coolness, determination and effect. And so it was on the present
occasion ... This stamps them as being no common burglars of the
usual criminal type ...* [15]

The indignation aroused by the Houndsditch murders soon became fury
and detestation. The police, acting on information received, had finally
traced Fritz and Sokolow to the room of Betsy Gershon on the second
floor of 100 Sidney Street. The fugitives were known to be armed and
dangerous. Through an informer, the police obtained a letter written by
Fritz to a contact in Courland, Russia, in which he gave a brief account
of the Houndsditch crime, proclaimed that he was innocent of shooting
policemen, that he believed the English police would hang him if they
caught him, and that consequently he was resolved to defend himself
against them and shoot himself in the last resort. In the light of events
two weeks earlier at Houndsditch, and in view of the resolution described
in Fritz's letter, the city police were entitled to regard themselves as
being in great danger should they attempt to arrest the two men at 100
Sidney Street. The room in which they were hiding was on the second
floor and was approached by a narrow stairway only wide enough for one
person at a time. The entrance to their room was around the corner of
the landing, which meant that a determined armed man could sweep the
stairway with automatic pistol fire without showing more of himself than
an arm and hand around the corner. A party of men proceeding up the
stairs could have been cut to pieces if caught in such a vulnerable
position. The police hoped to entice the men into the street by arranging
for their informer to offer them new hiding places, but the two
expropriators were wary and refused to take the chance. The authorities,
therefore, were in a quandary; they feared their quarry might yet escape
into the refugee community and submerge themselves completely. They
had no photographs of either Fritz or William, and only the vaguest of
descriptions. A failure to take the two men in Sidney Street could quite
easily mean a failure to take them at all.

Eventually it was decided that further delay was too risky. The two
men were known to be getting restless, Betsy Gershon was becoming
increasingly frightened of keeping them with her, and the police were
concerned that the men might easily slip through their fingers. They

resolved just before midnight on 3 January that the time had come to move in on Fritz and his companion. The haphazard manner in which subsequent events occurred indicates that the police had no clear strategy in mind. They made no attempt to arrest the men or to speak to them through an interpreter. There might have been little chance of any profit from such an attempt, but the possibility was never explored. The two fugitives were placed in a position of which they had no adequate understanding by a combination of mutual fear and distrust between themselves and the police, and their ignorance of British customs and institutions. Undoubtedly he was being wise after the event, but Detective-Inspector Wensley, who played a major role in all the subsequent proceedings, commented later that if Fritz Svaars and William Sokolow had only surrendered without a fight, they would probably have been acquitted of all complicity in the Houndsditch crime, as were some of the others, known to be far more directly involved. He went on to describe their resistance at Sidney Street as a wasteful tragedy that could easily have been avoided.[16] The police themselves, however, contributed to the tragedy by having no clearly worked-out plan of attack.

In the early hours of the morning of 4 January 1911 a small, well-armed group of policemen stole quietly into Sidney Street and sealed off the entire block in which 100 Sidney Street was situated. The police were armed with old-fashioned revolvers and a few with primitive morris-tube rifles, both weapons vastly inferior to the automatic mausers preferred by the Leesma men. Once officers had been posted at the rear of the building, in the building directly opposite, and at both ends of the block, police moved stealthily to the houses immediately adjacent and evacuated all residents. They then carefully and quietly woke the landlord and landlady of 100 Sidney Street in their ground floor rooms, and with their hesitant help managed to spirit the other lodgers and their children to safety. Betsy Gershon was tricked into coming downstairs and was quickly hustled away for interrogation. It was impossible that all this activity should have passed unnoticed. One of the tenants was an old man aged ninety-two who could not understand why he was being ordered by strangers to leave his warm bed and go out into the sleet and winter cold. He resisted violently and shouted in protest as he was unceremoniously thrust into his trousers and carried outside.

At this stage the police had closed off the street, secured the rear of the house and occupied the first two floors of 100 Sidney Street. And now they began to dither. What should they do next? The two desperadoes were probably awake, and it was thought to be too great a risk to attempt to mount the stairway and arrest them. Nor, apparently, was it feasible to obtain an interpreter and explain the position to the two men and call upon them to surrender. Instead, the police withdrew from the building, and as a wan and bleak winter's daylight slowly crept into the street, they bumbled about in front of the house, trying to decide on a course of action. Eventually, at about 7.30 am, it was decided to try and attract the wanted men's attention. Even then, no attempt was made at direct communication with them, but rather a police sergeant ran across the road to the front door and banged furiously on it before running back again. Nothing happened. Wensley next asked some of his men to throw stones at the windows of the second-floor room in which the men were thought to be. Still nothing happened. Then a policeman picked up a brick and flung it at the window. This at last produced a response. The window on the floor below was suddenly shattered and half a dozen shots were fired at the group of stone-throwing policemen opposite. They scattered in all directions, and one of them, Detective-Constable Leeson, received a shot in the chest, dangerously close to the heart. They all gained cover as shots ricocheted off the walls of the houses opposite 100 Sidney Street and flew up and down the street. Instead of being confined to one floor of the house by a police occupation of the ground and first floors, the two desperate men were given the run of the entire building. And the police had provoked the men to open fire on them. Their actions in abandoning the house to the men and then throwing stones at the windows and knocking on the door and running away can only be likened to those of small boys provoking a bully with taunts and stones from a position of imagined safety. The fugitives were never called upon to surrender, despite the fact that there was no shortage of Lettish interpreters available to the police. Continental newspapers, as reported in the columns of *The Times*, were later to make play of this slightly ridiculous behaviour by the police, and even *The Times*, while loyally extolling the bravery of police officers, was compelled to confess itself unable to understand how the men were to be captured by such methods. Riddling the house with bullets was not thought to be the most persuasive method of negotiating the surrender of armed ruffians.[17]

The hostilities proved easier to start than to stop, and the police quickly found that their antiquated weapons were no match for the powerful automatic mausers of the two Letts, who did not appear to be hampered by a shortage of ammunition as they sprayed the street and surrounding houses with bullets. Wensley, with Superintendent Mulvaney, requested Commissioner Woodhouse's permission to bring in troops from the Tower of London. This was a question beyond Woodhouse's jurisdiction and he telephoned the Home Secretary, Winston Churchill, who gave immediate authority for the police to use whatever force was necessary in the judgement of the men on the spot. Soon seventeen of the Scots Guards, under the command of a lieutenant and two NCOs, had drawn ammunition for their Lee Enfield rifles and were en route to Sidney Street. In the interim, reinforcements of police from surrounding divisions, armed with an assortment of revolvers, rifles and shotguns, had been arriving at the siege and joining in the exchange with the two men. Meanwhile, the incessant noise of continuous firing inevitably attracted a large and growing crowd of sightseers, who were often in danger of being hit by ricocheting bullets. As the crowd increased, so too did the number of policemen needed to control it and keep it back from a dangerous proximity to the action. By the end of the proceedings, early in the afternoon, it was estimated that there were almost 1000 police and soldiers involved in one capacity or another with the exciting events of the siege. The crowd by this time numbered many thousands, and plain-clothes police officers mingled in it, in case some attempt to rescue the two men was mounted by sympathizers amongst the large immigrant population present.

An enterprising reporter from the *Daily Chronicle* found himself a secure vantage point on the roof of a nearby public house and filed the following eyewitness report:

At both ends of Sidney Street the Scots Guards were in position, taking cover behind the angle of the houses. Around them were groups of policemen in uniform armed with shotguns, and numbers of plain clothes detectives with heavy revolvers. In the shadow of doorways and archways men crouched down with barrels of rifles and pistols pointed towards the house next to the doctor's surgery, with its shattered window-panes and broken brickwork. Looking down into the backyards of the houses opposite Martins-buildings, I could see soldiers and armed policemen moving about, climbing over fences, and getting up tall ladders, so that they could fire between the chimney pots.

On the roof of a great brewery on the same side of the way as the Rising Sun public house were scores of the work-people, and as far as the eye could see across the sloping roofs, the chimney-pots and parapets, the skyline was black with heads, while in the streets below, as far as a quarter of a mile away, there were vast and tumultuous crowds, kept back by lines of mounted policemen. The voices of those many thousands came up to me in great murmurous gusts, like the roar of wild beasts in a jungle. It seemed as if the whole of London had poured into Whitechapel and Stepney to watch one of the most deadly and thrilling dramas that has ever happened in the great city within living memory. [18]

By noon, a combination of the shrewd politician's inability to resist a crowd where reporters were present, and a curiosity to see the action at first-hand (or perhaps other reasons of high policy), had led to Winston Churchill's appearance on the scene. He was later to find this extremely embarrassing politically, and had to face charges both in parliament and in the press throughout the rest of January 1911 that he had shown immaturity and lack of judgement in becoming personally involved in the Sidney Street Siege, as well as a lack of that *gravitas* normally expected from a high-ranking member of His Majesty's government. A reporter who was at the siege later recounted his cynical amazement at Churchill's almost uncanny ability to move around during the operation so as always to be in front of the cameras. [19] Furthermore, the crowd gave Churchill a hostile reception as his car drove up, and the catcalls and abuse were in obvious allusion to the Liberal government's conviction that refugees seeking asylum from political and religious persecution should not be discriminated against when they sought sanctuary in Britain. It has already been noted that this view did not reflect the opinions of the majority of Anglo-Saxons in Whitechapel, and the locals took the opportunity to let the Home Secretary know the strength of their feelings. Churchill sensibly left the conduct of affairs to the men on the spot, but the myth was soon established that he had taken control of proceedings shortly after he arrived, and had personally directed operations against the two Letts from then on. If there were an element of truth in such a story the police could only have felt relief because the entire Sidney Street performance had been a fiasco.

A machine-gun was brought up, and artillery was sent for in an effort to break down the resistance of the two men. Fortunately for all concerned, the affair had ended by the time the horse-drawn guns arrived, and the machine-gun never actually opened fire. At 1 pm it was observed that the house had caught fire. Nobody knows how the fire broke out. It may have resulted from a stray bullet puncturing one of the gas pipes, or it may have been started deliberately by the men as a diversion to cover their attempted getaway, or as a last, defiant act of self-immolation. Whatever the reason, while the fire slowly took hold in the top story and then began to burn downwards, the fusillade of shots from the house continued unabated as the gunmen were slowly forced down to the ground floor. By mid-afternoon the house was a burnt-out shell. The fire brigade, whose had hitherto been forbidden by Winston Churchill to approach the blaze, were now permitted to set about extinguishing the flames and protecting the adjoining houses. It had been hoped that the inferno would eventually force the men into the street where they could be disposed of immediately. Their likely fate, had either man come into the street, was only too apparent at one stage of the fire when for a brief instant a burning curtain gave the appearance of a man crawling out onto the window ledge with his clothes in flames. This apparition was greeted by a prolonged and concentrated burst of firing from the besieging forces. In retrospect it is obvious that Fritz Svaars and William Sokolow were dead men from the time police evacuated the house and provoked them - either deliberately or through ineffectual leadership - into opening fire.

As police and salvage workers later sifted through the wreckage, they found the charred remains of two bodies, one with a bullet through the back of the head and the other killed by smoke suffocation. Three fire-affected automatic pistols were also discovered, and the authorities were then satisfied that they had accounted for the men primarily responsible for the deaths of the three policemen a few weeks earlier in Houndsditch. In this notion they were mistaken, but 'honour' had been satisfied in that the deaths of three policemen were quickly avenged by the deaths of three members of the gang who had murdered them.

The London newspapers took a supportive line over the siege and expressed gratification that the deaths of the two Letts had been accomplished without the loss of any more brave policemen. Detective-Constable Leeson was promoted to sergeant, awarded the King's medal for bravery, and recovered from his wound, whilst Winston Churchill defended his role in the House of Commons and through the letter columns of *The Times*. Abroad, however, the events of the siege did not meet with unalloyed admiration. The Germans commented acidly that it would not have taken over a thousand men to overpower two if the events had occurred in Germany; but it was left to the Irish to launch the most stinging attack. A report appeared in the *Constabulary Gazette*, the unofficial organ of the Royal Irish Constabulary, which was headed 'Police Funk in London', and read in part:

It is to be hoped that Scotland Yard and the Home Office authorities feel as small as they look after the farce that was enacted by them in the metropolis on Tuesday last. Fifteen hundred armed policemen, two companies of Guards, a Gatling Gun, and Mr Churchill, all engaged in attempting to capture a couple of common-place burglars whose motto was 'do not hesitate to shoot'. We have heard an immense amount of talk recently about the brave police of London, alleged to be the best force in the world, but in this paltry affair they have cut a sorry figure. The police were actually within the building, and removed all the occupants except the burglars. They then decamped, threw stones at the windows to awaken the occupants, and proceeded then to call out the fighting forces of the Empire. When the house caught fire they not only declined to extinguish the flames but turned a hose of scalding steam into it, so as to ensure the helplessness of the men inside. The next time they find themselves suffering from funk in London, if they will send us a wireless message we promise to send them a phalanx of Irish boys who will capture their men without firing a shot. Had somebody got on the roof there are scores of suffocating mixtures that might have been dropped down the chimney, and thus the culprits might have been captured alive. It is not the duty of a police officer to inflict punishment.[20]

FOOTNOTES

1   The Special Branch report forms part of a large collection of papers from the City of London police force dealing with the Houndsditch murders in December 1910. They are now in the Guildhall Records Office, London, and will be referred to hereafter as the Houndsditch Papers.

2   Houndsditch Papers.

3   ibid. This estimate of fifteen is accepted by the only author to have made use of the police records. *See* Donald Rumbelow, op. cit., p. 39.

4   *Rankpelnis*, 30 December 1910.

5   Houndsditch Papers. Although I have given only one alias to each of these men, they seemed to change names regularly, and each one had a list of alternative names and nicknames by which he was known. These will be reproduced in full in the Rogues' Gallery, and I will use their most common names in the main text of the book. Names in the revolutionary movement meant very little; they were changed as often and as readily as an overcoat.

6   *The Times*, 25 January 1909. *See also* more comment in the same vein in *The Times*, 26 January 1909. The other organs of the popular press in London were less restrained in their attitudes and coverage.

7   *Hansard's Parliamentary Debates*, 5th series, 25 February 1909, cols 971-2, and 1 March 1909, cols 1103-4.

8   Fritz's letter in Houndsditch Papers.

9   William J. Fishman, op. cit., p. 264.

10 Houndsditch Papers.

11 Houndsditch Papers. The entire reconstruction of the Houndsditch crime and the Sidney Street siege which followed are based upon this complete and extensive set of police records, unless otherwise indicated in the footnotes.

12 This man has been clearly identified as Jacob Peters, but contemporary accounts mistook him for Gardstein. See Rumbelow, op. cit., pp. 142-52.

13 Martin's cowardice has only recently come to light. See Rumbelow, op. cit., p. 57.

14 *Report of Inquest on December 20th, 1910, and on the 6th January 1911 and the 3rd and 10th days of February 1911, at the City Coroner's Court, concerning the death of Police Sergeant Robert Bentley*. City 1911, no. 26.

15 *The Times*, 19 December 1910. All the popular London dailies made the same point as had *The Times*, that the criminals were obviously foreigners.

16 Frederick P. Wensley, *Detective Days: The Record of Forty-two Years' Service in the Criminal Investigation Department*, London, 1931, p. 167.

17 *The Times*, 4 January 1911.

18 *Daily Chronicle*, 4 January 1911.

19 *Sunday Telegraph*, 23 January 1966.

20 The *Constabulary Gazette*, 7 January 1911.

3
SPIES, INFORMERS AND THE BRITISH RESPONSE

The amateur quality characteristic of police conduct during the siege of Sidney Street similarly pervaded the investigations of the Houndsditch murders. There seems little doubt that had one of the gang not accidentally been shot, the investigation by the City of London police could not have proceeded. Moreover, the unexpected and extreme violence had produced a sense of shock throughout the force. After all, as *The Times* had been quick to point out, British criminals just did not behave in so disagreeable a manner:

For one of the curious things about the regular criminals is the absence of any grudge against the police, who are regarded as only doing their duty and engaged in a fair match of wits and nimbleness. A savage delight in taking life is the mark of the modern Continental anarchist criminal. We have our own ruffians, but we do not breed that type here, and we do not want them. It may be impossible to keep them out, but it is quite possible to discourage them more effectually than we do. They receive a negative if not a positive welcome; things are made easy for them, and they like to come here in preference to their native land or other Continental countries, not because our police are less efficient, but because they have inadequate powers. Why should we harbour known foreign criminals as we do? Why should our police be compelled to tackle these murderous scoundrels under conditions which permit them to be all shot down one after another, while the assassins escape?[1]

In addition to some form of shock paralysing and inhibiting the police investigations, however, sheer inefficiency also played a part. As Donald Rumbelow has clearly shown, the authorities so hopelessly bungled the ballistics report relating to the murders at Houndsditch that the real murderer, Jacob Peters, escaped scot-free, whilst the luckless trio of George Gardstein, Fritz Svaars and William Sokolow were saddled with responsibility for the crime.[2] Events had conspired fortuitously to present the police with three corpses, and they seemed almost anxious to decide that these were also the bodies of the men most heavily involved in the killing of Tucker, Bentley and Choat. Unpleasant questions concerning the events in Sidney Street could be swept under the carpet if the two fugitives killed there could be condemned posthumously as murderers. Moreover, it was a solution with intrinsic appeal to a tidy mind and embodying a rough sort of natural justice.

The murders appear to have produced a sense of genuine outrage in the public mind, and the police correspondence files were choked with letters offering helpful suggestions to assist the police in their enquiries. The newspapers took an active part in keeping the public informed about the progress of the investigation whilst at the same time indulging in an orgy of speculation concerning the *émigré* community in London's East End, replete with commentary on the difficulties faced by police attempting to conduct a murder inquiry in an environment where people had closed ranks fearfully against outsiders. The police files also show, however, that on occasion domestic disputes were dragged in to confuse the situation. One woman, for example, wrote to inform the police of her belief that her husband was involved in the murders. Her disaffection emerged later in the letter, when she trenchantly commented that if the authorities wanted to interview him he could always be found in the local public house.[3] The files indicate a widespread interest in the progress of the investigation and suggest that Britain was full of suspicious-looking foreigners who exactly matched the vague descriptions of the Leesma expropriators that had been circulated to the newspapers by the city police.

In addition to the self-congratulatory way in which British newspapers commented upon the fact that - in a turbulent and dangerous age - Englishmen were not as other men, there was also a latent infatuation with those very characteristics of impetuosity and belligerence which commentators attributed so readily to other Europeans. The acceptance of the stereotype of the Englishman as law-abiding and politically phlegmatic may help to explain the press's excessive interest in crimes of violence both at home and abroad. It was something of a paradox, permitting the British to feel superior to those individuals who were perhaps living out the fantasies of their observers.

The killings seemed to bring out the best and the worst in people's characters. As well as informing on their families, friends and acquaintances, many volunteered further, more detailed assistance. One crazed psychotic from Oxford penned a series of lengthy and illegible diatribes to the police attempting to prove the existence of an international red brotherhood of anarchists which had spread its tentacles into every country in Europe and subverted all executive government with secret agents. The alleged master-minds behind the British operation were his sister-in-law and his niece, Annie and Charlotte Bilderbeck.[4] Another equally inventive soul named Richard Lee sought notoriety by claiming to have been involved in the Houndsditch crime and to have been an eyewitness to the shootings. His account of the crime amounted to imaginative farce, with a gang leader named Jack and a woman accomplice called Poll.[5] Yet another would-be assistant was an expatriate Australian who apparently had gone insane and was convinced that his long-lost daughter - missing since the age of six - was either Luba Milstein or Sara Trassjonsky. He agitated privately and publicly for an opportunity to confront his missing daughter, and his letters bear the filing clerk's notation that he was 'soft in the head'.[6]

In addition to informing police whenever some hapless foreigner was sighted, other members of the public tried to be helpful by offering constructive suggestions concerning the best methods to be adopted during the inquiries. One writer advised the police to appeal for help to the schoolteachers in all East End public schools, since the children would undoubtedly be talking about the Houndsditch murders and many important clues could be discovered as to the whereabouts of the men in hiding. The teachers should be requested to eavesdrop on playground and lunch-time conversations, and to report anything noteworthy or out of the ordinary. Another correspondent proposed that the police should set up a fake emigration office in the East End. Plain-clothes detectives could pose as emigration agents offering free passages to a selection of those countries anarchist assassins were known to favour when they were on the run. A third suggestion was that police should organize a fake funeral for George Gardstein and have all the mourners shadowed when the funeral service was completed. Yet another man warned the authorities to check the large laundry trolleys that took clean linen aboard ships preparing to sail. The anarchists could make good their escape by hiding in the laundry.[7]

Such suggestions were imaginative, and some of them might have born fruit had the police been possessed of the unlimited reserves of manpower necessary for their implementation. There were, however, other offers of help forthcoming which relied more on the supernatural than the everyday perception and intelligence of ordinary men and women. Some people thought that important clues concerning the whereabouts of Peter the Painter and other members of the terrorist organization could be garnered from their dreams. Mr Thomas White wrote excitedly to the police only a few days after the Houndsditch killings to announce that in a dream his wife had discovered the hideout of the wanted men 'down a lane at the back of the Pavilion Theatre near the side entrance'. Mrs White was not the only inspired dreamer to offer help to the police. Another letter on file relates a similar experience: 'I have had a marvellous dream and I think you will find the leader of the Gang that shot the Police on the Continent a Female personating [sic] a French soldier with small round military hat and long false black whiskers. She has an abundant of Black Hair dressed high on the head when in female dress'. A third offer of psychic help came from Patrick J. Todd who mailed a letter to the police on Christmas day in which he informed them that 'the man you have arrested is the one who has committed the murder'. Since the authorities had arrested two men by this stage, Osip Federoff and Jacob Peters, the advice was not particularly helpful. Todd had a preoccupation with retribution, and in a series of letters expressed his hopes that both the men and the women arrested would be punished severely. He claimed Sara Trassjonsky was an experienced revolutionary and not the simple girl that she appeared, and he informed the police, 'I have foretold other things in my past life - do as I say you will be alright ... I am the truth adviser I don't tell a lie to any person. If I would I would have a sin to answer'.[8]

Not all the psychics were so improbable and harmless. Mrs Rose Sloggett addressed a whole series of letters to the police attempting to link her employers - two foreign gentlemen - with the Leesma group and international anarchism. To this end she claimed psychic powers and astrological knowledge, and offered the authorities her assistance provided they kept it secret from her husband who disapproved of her powers and had already threatened to leave her. She was obviously deranged, and her letters were a farrago of prejudice against foreigners and fear of being stabbed with a sword-stick owned by her employers. Not so easy to dispose of, however, was the man who put his medium, Esther, into an hypnotic trance and in several letters to the police gave an apparently detailed account of the activities of Peter the Painter as he made his way to the docks and escaped by sea to Europe. The police did not pay much attention to these accounts, but they are the most rational of all the psychic help proffered and may be the only suggestions about what happened to Peter the Painter following his disappearance. Unfortunately, Esther rather spoiled her record and compromised her powers by informing the police shortly afterwards that she had once again gone into a trance and 'seen' Peter the Painter returning to England hell-bent on a new mission to assassinate Winston Churchill.[9]

The personality of Peter Piaktow began to loom like a colossus in the mind of the general public, and letters on the police file illustrate this growing preoccupation with Peter and a degree of admiration for his cleverness at evading capture. One measure of his impact lay in the number of letters filed purporting to have been written by him. Mostly these came from correspondents who were barely literate and apparently shared nothing in common other than a sneaking admiration for a man who could successfully defy the entire London police force. No two of these letters are in the same handwriting, and they probably betoken nothing more than a latent hostility towards the police and an enjoyment in seeing the forces of law and order discomforted. (At the time of the Jack the Ripper murders, thirty years before, the London police received several letters from correspondents claiming to be the Ripper himself.) The first contact from any of these self-declared Peter the Painters appears to have been a telegramme received by police on 30 December 1910. This cable is registered on the cover sheet of one of the correspondence files, but it is missing from the file itself. Early in January 1911 two letters were written. They were sent respectively to the London chief of police, and to the editor of the *Daily Mirror*. The chief of police's letter was postmarked Manchester and is typical of the barely literate correspondence in this category. All these letters are distinguished by an interest in violence and bloodshed.

Chief of Police

Sir,

You perhaps think as you have outwitted peter [sic] do you but I don't think as you have. You had best take care of your Van when riding up to police station with your prisoners for it shall not be our falt [sic] if they are not shot or you constebles [sic] are. We mean to show you what foreignurs [sic] are mad [sic] of not counting flowing blood. We mean 'KILL'. So be prepared. I am here in Manchester safe and sound enough reward of £500 will not be enough to what I have given others for a secret hiding pl. We will have that bloddy [sic] swine of a Churchill before ere long the days are numbered. You will have to notice all London have their horror [sic] ere long not only one struk [sic]. We are a strong party.

Yours, Peters.[10]

The letter to the editor of the *Daily Mirror* was postmarked Battersea: 'We wish to let you know that before we are finished we shall blow up and destroy all the stores in London.' This one was signed 'Perter the Painter'. Another similar letter to the police was despatched on 14 January 1911 in which 'Peter' informed the authorities that they would need more than 1500 policemen to catch him. On 6 February 'Peter' sent a postcard 'Sir, I'm still in London', whilst on 28 April he and Fritz Svaars challenged the police to find them.

Sir,

You know we are still alive and kicking. We shall be round the meat market tomorrow so be on the look out for us. You think your [sic] clever but you can't catch us.

signed by
Peter the Painter and Fritz

Excuse the note paper.[11]

These letters are proof that some people, at least, thoroughly enjoyed the mortification of the authorities and gloried in the fact that the real Peter the Painter remained at large. In addition to amusement there is an undercurrent of hostility towards property and a desire to see the police humiliated. Obviously Peter the Painter appealed to some atavistic streak, and the myth of the daring and resourceful will-o'-the-wisp seems to have been established in these early weeks after the siege of Sidney Street. This conception received constant reinforcement during the following years as reports reached the police claiming that Peter had been sighted in Amsterdam, Antwerp, Brussels, Finland, Italy, Germany, Switzerland, South Africa, Canada and Australia.

It was not just amongst Englishmen that echoes from Houndsditch and Sidney Street reverberated. The *émigré* community took a close interest in the affair and was very conscious of the hundreds of plain-clothes detectives attempting to pass themselves off as immigrants. The Houndsditch crime received wide coverage in the newspapers of Europe, and letters were received from Russia which seemed to indicate that overseas opinion was as divided as British. A letter arrived from S. Dueranbi of St Petersburg which reproduced the frankly celebratory tone of the Peter the Painter correspondence already noted, and threatened 'very bad trouble' if the English police persisted with their search for the missing Peter. To reinforce his point, Dueranbi had drawn a pistol on the back of his letter and labelled it 'the Maurir'. On the other hand, however, there was also a telegramme forwarded to Scotland Yard from the Society of the United Russians in Novgorod which expressed senti-ments precisely the opposite of those espoused by Dueranbi. 'Grieving nearly every day over members of our Russian Police killed by the anarchist Jews we deeply sympathize now with the sorrow caused to the police force under your control. We hope by our united efforts to at last get rid of these murdering Jews.'[12]

This hostility to Jews also emerged in a letter from the king's procu-rator, Antwerp, when he wrote requesting copies of the descriptions of the wanted men and photographs of Peter Piaktow: 'We have in fact, in our town an important Jewish colony, where for several years there are numerous suspicious elements, a certain number of whom seem to be in constant relation with the Jews in London.'[13] Jewish hatred of tsarism was a widely appreciated phenomenon, both inside and outside Russia, and the measure of co-operation between the Jewish Bund and the other revolutionary groups in exile was no secret.

Orthodox Jews were easier to identify than many other nationalities, but nationalistic prejudice in Europe was by no means restricted to them alone. Any visibly foreign person was likely to come under police scrutiny, especially if he seemed to behave furtively and to be of Eastern European extraction. There is ample evidence that European police forces co-operated assiduously with London in attempts to track down the murderers. The following account illustrates not only the lengths to which continental police authorities were prepared to go in their quest for information, but also the major difficulty they faced in their attempts to regulate the behaviour of a group of men who led the itinerant life of many young anti-tsarist revolutionaries. The letter is from the minister of justice, Brussels, and is dated 4 February 1911. It reads in part,

My attention has been drawn to a stranger of Russian nationality who
arrived at Brussels about 12 days ago and staying at the Hotel de
Calais, No. 12 Avenue Fonsny, St Gilles, where he registered under
the name of Jean Leonard de Felita-Mosonivel, born at Varsovie, age
27 years, Doctor of Medicine. Since his arrival at this hotel, this
individual, who only speaks Russian and German, keeps to his room
under the pretence that he is ill and passes his days in reading and
smoking.
   He is destitute of baggage and money and does not possess papers of
identity. To a special officer instructed to obtain information
respecting him, he declared that his correct name is Jean-Leonard
Morozewicz born at Putrake (Poland, Russia) the 7th September 1885.
   He continued his confidences in adding that he had come from
Paris, where he had stayed a fortnight coming from London, and that
he had been obliged to leave Paris because he was a Russian terrorist.
   He also declared that two years ago he was wanted by the Police of
Varsovie for the terrorist outrage at Nargrafski in which he was
implicated with twenty of his compatriots, that he should have suffered
eight months of detention at Varsovie. Released and re-arrested three
weeks afterwards escaped and he went successfully to New York,
Cairo, Alexandria, Las Palmas, London, and finally to Paris . . . [14]

The Houndsditch and Sidney Street affairs inevitably brought all non-British nationals in London under intense public scrutiny. So oppressive was this close attention that many Europeans resident in the metropolis found it politic to dissociate themselves from any hint of sympathy with the perpetrators of so abhorrent a crime. The Swiss Institute approached the police to express the repugnance of their members for such a violation of the hospitality England traditionally extended to foreigners of all nations. They declared their appreciation of the gallantry and courtesy of the London police who so often helped foreigners find their way through the streets of Europe's biggest city, and they forwarded three guineas for the fund established for the wives and dependants of the murdered officers.
   The various political organizations in the refugee community were also quick to disavow the crime. The Social Democratic Party, the Socialist Revolutionaries, and the more philosophical of the anarchists all made strenuous attempts to ensure that they could not be accused of complicity with the criminals, and the police press releases show that the authorities were more than happy to co-operate in such an attempt. If the political basis of the attempted robbery were accepted, then those involved might not have been subject to deportation were they to be found guilty in a court of law. Thus the police appeared to be content to accept the specious self-serving arguments of the political spokesmen that the crime was in no sense political, despite the fact that their private reports and notations on correspondence received show that they were

not deceived and were cognizant of the political realities which underlay
the murders and the siege of Sidney Street.

The xenophobic popular press had a field day. Papers were full of
revelations concerning the alleged corruption and endemic violence
throughout the East End immigrant community. Even *The Times* capitulated to prejudice and delivered a broadside against the governments of
Turkey, Greece, Russia and Italy, for permitting the emigration of
political undesirables to Britain.[15] The next day, the consul general
for Greece contacted Scotland Yard, pointedly asking whether it was
really the experience of the police that Greece was one of the countries
from which such undesirables chiefly came. The commissioner's reply
conceded that Greece did not seem to produce many trouble-makers in
the area under his responsibility, but went on to point out that the city
police force was only accountable for law and order within the confines
of the one square mile that made up 'the City'. Beyond that area was the
responsibility of the metropolitan police force, and since that force dealt
with all crime in the greater London districts which lay outside 'the
City', their experience with Greeks would be of such an order as to
permit an official comment on the consul general's question.[16]

In addition to the letters offering help to the police, there was another
large collection expressing horror, shock and detestation of criminals,
together with sympathy for the dependants of the three dead policemen.
A public subscription was quickly organized and more than £2000 was
collected for this worthy cause. The immense crowd which gathered
outside St Paul's Cathedral on 23 December 1910 to witness the public
funeral of the three policemen gave some indication of the degree to
which this tragedy had touched the hearts of ordinary English men and
women. Similarly, the volume of correspondence expressing sorrow and
enclosing offerings towards the subscription further reinforces the view
that the killings at Houndsditch and the affray in Sidney Street affected
many members of the general public in an unusually personal way.

One intriguing facet of this second mass of correspondence was that it
appeared to come predominantly from a different sector of society than
had the offers of help and the suggestions previously noted. As a rule, the
letters of sympathy and condolence were well written, grammatical and
legible; they were often on embossed note paper and for the most part
were accompanied by business or calling cards. Sorrow at the deaths of
the policemen was rarely expressed by the other letters, which tended to
be barely literate, ungrammatical, scrawled on odd bits of paper and
unaccompanied by cards or return addresses.

The impact of the shootings at Houndsditch and Sidney Street was
immense. Two women at least were driven insane. On 22 December 1910
the London police were notified that

*A woman giving the name of Maud Belinsky, age 35, speaks English
well, but declines to give address or other particulars is today detained*

in St George's Infirmary Fulham Road as a lunatic suffering from the delusion that the men who shot the Police in the City are going to shoot her, and that she can see men going about with revolvers about to shoot the Police.[17]

63
SPIES, IN-
FORMERS
AND THE
BRITISH
RESPONSE

The second female to lose her mind as a result of these crimes was one of the participants, Sara Trassjonsky, whose reason failed under the pressure of imprisonment added to the stress of tending the dying George Gardstein and a lifetime of pain and privation. Shortly after the court case Sara was incarcerated in Colney Hatch Asylum as a patient who had become hopelessly insane. The police files contain little further mention of her, except a notation that she was reported to be insane with suicidal tendencies, and that the prognosis for any sort of recovery was extremely poor.[18]

Not all the sorrow and indignation was genuine, however, or at least it was not permitted to cloud good business acumen. Early in January 1911 Mr Henry J. Derby, a former chief inspector in the metropolitan police, approached the commissioner of police for the City of London on behalf of Madame Tussaud's Waxworks. The waxworks proposed to exhibit models of the murdered police officers. This proposal is further evidence of the intensity of public interest in the affair, and Derby had been retained to approach the authorities and to ascertain whether major objections would be raised. Sir William Nott Bower, the Commissioner, made his displeasure extremely obvious and Madame Tussaud's dropped the suggestion very quickly.[19]

Madam Tussaud's was not the only attempt to wring a measure of commercial profit from the tragic deaths of the three policemen, although it was the crassest endeavour to do so. The agents for the sale of Mauser automatic pistols in Britain were quick to take advantage of the opportunity and contacted the authorities pointing out that until the police were equipped with weapons equal to those favoured by terrorists, such unhappy occurrences could not really be avoided. They offered to demonstrate Mausers to the commissioner of police and were hopefully anticipating a large order. Indeed, there was a major flow of mail to the city police of a commercial or semi-commercial kind, and there were various suggestions for the manufacture of ammonia bombs to flush malfactors out of hiding, or of ether and chloroform bombs to render them unconscious. One man added a distinctively Australian flavour by advising that police on anti-terrorist duty be equipped with suits of thick armour modelled on that worn by 'the bushranger Ned Kelly'. One firm of surgical limb suppliers sent along a catalogue of their artificial legs and arms with an indication that they would be more than willing to attempt the manufacture of jointed body armour for members of the police force.[20]

·Another area in which people sought a personal return from the crime was in the appointment of interpreters. Because the murders and the siege had involved aliens rather than the native English population, it was clear that interpreters would be required who were conversant with Yiddish, Russian and other eastern European languages. The files contain a number of letters from immigrants offering their services and claiming an intimate acquaintance with the East End and its inhabitants. One letter came from a former employee of the *Daily Mail* newspaper who claimed to have done extensive interpreting work as part of his newspaper career. Moreover, he had special contacts in the East End:

I have done a lot of work for the Jews in the vicinity of Grove St. I know the whole of the locality well and one person in particular known as the 'King of the Boys' is very friendly inclined towards me. This man lives in Ellen St and knows everybody and all that is to be known. [21]

The venal motive reared its head in other less innocent connections. The police records are voluminous, and they make it abundantly clear that refugees within the East End community were quickly in touch with the police offering to assist in the apprehension of the wanted men and women for money; the police were inundated with *émigrés* offering to turn in their friends and acquaintances for a reward. Police investigations would have been quite fruitless had it not been for the active co-operation of men who undertook to betray their compatriots for a gratuity. The early arrests of Osip Federoff and Jacob Peters were the direct result of information passed to the police by a young balalaika player named Nicolai Tomacoff. Tomacoff had been well connected with many of the Leesma group through the Jubilee Street Anarchist Club, and had actually been in Peter the Painter's room at 59 Grove Street when the final briefing session took place on Friday 16 December 1910. Because he was not one of the Leesma organization, the group delayed the briefing until he had departed, but he was still able to provide the authorities with a list of names, descriptions and addresses. In return, the police showered him with small gifts of clothing, hotel accommodation and trips around London's suburbs, whilst Tomacoff hunted out those members of Leesma group 5 about whom he had some knowledge. [22]

Other immigrants also attempted to bargain with the police and offered information in return for money. Theodore Jansen was only one of many who tried this, and as a result of his chicanery his temporary lodger Karl Hoffman was eventually arrested. The published accounts of this episode which occurred on 7 February 1911, show that the city police were aware that Hoffman was an extremely dangerous man and were determined that the farcical proceedings of Sidney Street would not be repeated. *The Times* commented approvingly on the improvement in official technique.

The methods employed were at first similar to those at Sidney Street. In this case a neighbour was asked to rouse the house-holder. This man

Peter Piaktow 'Peter the Painter'

Group of unidentified émigrés *with August Maren far right*

Unidentified Leesma terrorist posing with automatic pistol

L to R: Karl Hoffman, Jacob Fogel, Bifsteks

John Rosen

Ernest Dreger

Jacob Peters

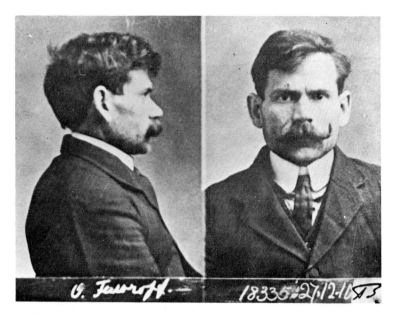

Osip Federoff

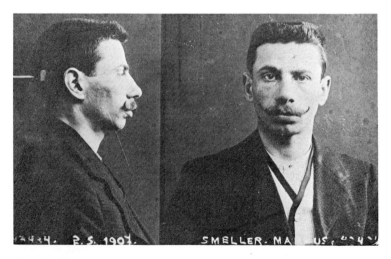

Max Smoller

Karl Hoffman

Nina Vassilleva

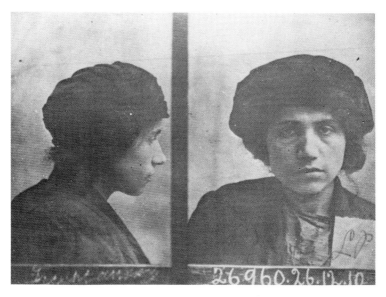

Sara Trassjonsky

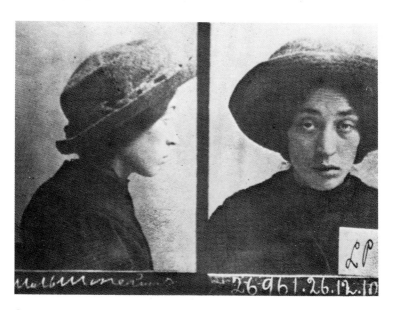

Luba Milstein

Yourka Dubof

August Maren in white hat

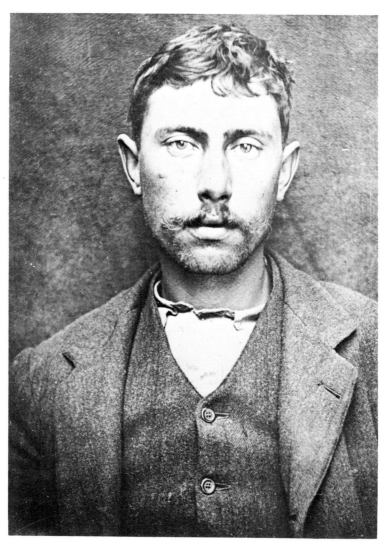

Frederick Johnson

*crept along the flat roof of the shop front and knocked at the
hairdresser's bedroom window. After some parley the police were
admitted by the back of the premises. Then the front was opened and a
systematic clearance of the inmates made. Detective-inspectors
Wensley, Willis and Newall conducted the search of the interior. In
the ground-floor back the man upon whom suspicion centred was
found fast asleep. His host and hostess and their child were silently
removed. There was no retiring to throw gravel at the windows this
time. The officers pounced upon the sleeping man and secured him
. . . Although the detained man pretended that he had no knowledge
of the Houndsditch affair, it appears that he is known to be an intimate
associate of 'Peter the Painter'.*[23]

Ironically, Theodore Jansen had recently had another temporary lodger
who had expressed great interest in the crimes and who had been a
member of the wider Leesma organization. This man used the nickname
Yahnit (Johnny or Little John) and was destined to play a major role in
the ensuing events. It was *this* man whom Jansen had attempted to
betray, but the police missed him and caught the much bigger fish in
Karl Hoffman. The authorities noted on the bottom of one of Jansen's
many statements that he had asked for money every time he came to see
them and that he was not to be trusted. Jansen received no money for his
activities and the police found themselves playing cat and mouse with a
man they regarded as totally unreliable.

Many other immigrants made statements to the police in which they
volunteered to turn informer for pecuniary recompense, but there were
other more sinister informers at large within the refugee community: the
secret agents of the Ochrana. It has already been noted that the Ochrana
had adopted a policy of infiltrating all the anti-tsarist groups, and the
Leesma terrorists seem to have been no exception. In such cases the
difficulty normally lay in determining which group members were
actually tsarist spies. In this case, however, there is a firm indication that
such an agent did exist, that he was operating with the full knowledge
and consent of the Russian government, and that his identity was such a
closely guarded secret that the Russian consul general himself acted as
interpreter when the British police and the Russian spy agreed to meet.
The evidence of this claim lies in a letter from the Russian consulate to
Superintendent John Ottaway of the detective department, City of
London police, on 30 January 1911.

Dear Mr Ottaway,

*I received from that gentleman, whom I introduced to you, when he
was in London, a letter asking me to tell you that any direct relations
of the Police with that other gentleman, whom you know, must be
stopped. Therefore I should be very much obliged if you would arrange*

that no direct intercourse of that sort would take place. That person must not call upon you or at the Police Station and no Police Officer should call upon him. The only way would be to arrange interviews at public places, like railway stations, restaurants and so forth. If my services, as confidential interpreter, are needed, I am at your disposal, but again only under the circumstances as above.

I am, Dear Mr Ottaway,

Yours faithfully,
Consul General[24]

Such a letter indicates not only the existence of a secret Russian agent on the case, but also that his immediate superior in the field was not resident in London. If, as seems likely, the foreign agency of the Ochrana had an interest in the Houndsditch and Sidney Street affairs, one would not expect the officer in charge of the operation to visit London unless matters were coming to a head. At that stage, he would arrive and negotiate with the British authorities through the official representative of his government. The tone of the letter is also illustrative in that the consul general feels free to direct British detectives in a forthright and somewhat pre-emptory manner. It is the letter of a man who feels secure and in control of the situation. The note mentioned by the consul general refers to correspondence from the agent's superior who has returned to the continent, whilst the 'other gentleman' is a reference to the local agent. It is known that the police received information concerning the hideout of Fritz Svaars and William Sokolow from an immigrant whose identity they went to extraordinary lengths to protect. His name is never mentioned in the files and police reports where he is referred to always as 'a certain person'. It was only by the sheerest coincidence that some important clues to his identity emerged from the landlady of Sidney Street during an inquiry established to recommend compensation for those innocent residents of the house who had lost everything they possessed in the fire at the culmination of the siege. In that inquiry Mrs Fleishman testified that the house had been visited two days before the siege by a gentleman,

who wore a cap and a Chester [loose overcoat] and boots with leggings on, but he had a little parcel under his arm; it was simply like an umbrella, but it was a long thing and it was white and covered with American cloth carried under his arm. I says 'Whom do you want?' He says 'I want Mrs Gershaw,' and I was telling a lie to say Mrs Gershaw had gone to work, when she called down and came down from the second to the first floor and said 'Mrs Fleishman let him up, he is a photographer,' and I let him up, and he might have been there from a quarter past two till about ten minutes to three when he came down and I watched him again . . . [25]

It is the combination of the profession of the visitor with the police notes pencilled while actually in conference with the secret informer that establishes fairly conclusively that this local Ochrana agent was Charles Perelman, the original landlord of many of the Leesma people when the group first began to assemble in London.[26] What better occupation for a member of the secret police responsible for keeping the activities of the Leesma terrorists under observation and forewarning his superiors of the group's plans?

It is probable that Perelman tipped off the Russian authorities about Karl Hoffman and Fritz Svaars when they both returned clandestinely to Russia between 1909 and the end of 1910. Information supplied to the British police showed that Hoffman had been shadowed by the Russian police who surrounded the house in which he was staying. With great difficulty he succeeded in escaping from this ambush and regained sanctuary in Britain. Similarly, Fritz Svaars was placed under surveillance by the police when he returned to Russia, but he was unable to avoid capture and brutal interrogation. In a letter he wrote to his sister, he describes a series of beatings dealt out by the Russian police during this period.[27] Fritz broke down under this interrogation and gave information to the police. He then escaped to London again, though his wife and sister remained in Russia. It is possible that Fritz became a reluctant double agent at this time, and that the safety of his wife and sister were purchased by his agreement to keep the Ochrana informed regarding the London activities of the Lettish revolutionaries. It was established Ochrana practice to arrange 'escapes' for their newly converted agents, so that the traitors returned to their organizations as heroes rather than under suspicion.[28] Certainly, Fritz Svaars's behaviour fits the role of informer, and it does provide an explanation for the activities of that other enigmatic personality Peter the Painter. It may also explain Fritz's anxiety to send money to his wife sufficient for her to join him in London and from there to emigrate together to a place described by Fritz as 'the blessed land of Australia', where such murky proceedings could be forgotten and life begun anew. The letter Fritz wrote on the eve of the Sidney Street siege shows that his mind was preoccupied with getting away to Australia with his wife. Moreover, he protested his innocence in the matter of the Houndsditch killings, and his account of what had happened there and of George Gardstein being brought to his rooms in Grove Street agrees with the known facts of the case. What the letter failed to mention, an omission that could be very significant, was his relationship with Peter Piaktow.

All contemporary accounts agree that the two men were very close once Peter arrived in London from Europe towards the end of 1910. Fritz's mistress, Luba Milstein, found Fritz's reliance on Piaktow baffling and upsetting. Fritz made it plain to her that Piaktow was terribly important to him, and even gave him one of the two rooms they rented in Grove Street. There is no indication of any earlier meeting between the two men, and most of those outside the Leesma group found Peter reserved.[29] Nevertheless, it was in his room that the briefing session was held prior to the attempt on Harris's jewellery shop, and it was in his room also that the political meetings of the various Lettish groups opposed to the tsar were held. It is a measure of Piaktow's ability as a manager of men, that he could involve the Lettish Social Democrats, the Socialist Revolutionaries, and the anarchists in co-ordinated expropriations. These groups normally distrusted one another and preferred to work independently. Between the two of them, however, Fritz and Peter managed to involve all the Lettish terrorist groups in the Leesma organization. And this sort of co-ordination was a prerequisite if the Ochrana's *agents provocateurs* were to attempt to discredit the entire revolutionary movement in Britain, with the ultimate aim of ensuring the alteration and weakening of Britain's traditional policy of offering sanctuary to all political refugees. Fritz and Peter did their work extraordinary well.

Again, there is the question of finance. What did the two men live on? Luba Milstein once asked Fritz and was curtly ordered to mind her own business. Peter did not work whilst he was in London, nor did Fritz in the months leading up to December 1910, yet the three of them apparently paid their rent regularly and ate well enough. They did not need to pawn the sewing machine or the furniture as did most immigrants when prolonged bouts of unemployment overtook them. Fritz was even able to send £60 to his wife to cover her fare to London and both their fares to Australia. Where did this money come from? Donald Rumbelow suggests that Fritz and Luba were living on the proceeds of previous robberies,[30] but if that were so, then why increase the financial burden by taking in a stranger like Peter Piaktow, and why permit him to gain such an ascendancy in the relationship? Luba sensed Peter's power over Fritz and loathed him for it. She could not comprehend how a man of action like Fritz could so surrender his will to a man like Piaktow.

These difficulties can be resolved if we presume that Fritz Svaars had turned double agent, and that the mysterious source of finance was the Ochrana, who also introduced Peter Piaktow to control and assist the luckless Fritz. Peter appears to have been a clever and trusted agent for the secret police who was placed with the Judas figure of Fritz to assist in the downfall of the Lettish revolutionaries in London. Peter's history, insofar as it is known, shows that he had travelled throughout Europe and was personally familiar with nearly every country on the continent. The profile British police assembled on this man shows that Peter Piaktow was an alias. He came from Baltic Russia, from the Province of Courland, district of Goldingen, and his name was thought to be Evan Evanovitch (Janis Janisoff) Jakle alias Jaklis. He had been born on 19 July 1883. He had a brother and four sisters, and the family lived on a farm named Kounen in the district of Talsen. He was wanted by the police for absconding and evading military service. He had been imprisoned for acts committed during the 1905 Revolution, but 'escaped'. He lived for some time in France before surfacing in England, and his power over Fritz Svaars - an experienced and hardened revolutionary - and the details of his stay in London are shrouded in mystery. The relationship and behaviour of the two men begins to make sense if we regard them as *agents provocateurs* for the tsarist authorities. A reluctant spy like Fritz had limited use, and the Ochrana ruthlessly sacrificed him once he had outlived his usefulness. His spirited fight at Sidney Street is explicable in terms of a return to direct action by a man purging his guilt and striking back at police and authorities who had blackmailed him into betraying his comrades. It was also the last stand of a man who must have known that his bosses had sold him out to the British. Certainly his fellow conspirators seem to have been uneasy about him. His cousin Jacob Peters bitterly blamed Fritz for the entire affair, whilst Osip Federoff likened him to the notorious double agent Azeff who ran the terrorist wing of the Socialist Revolutionaries for several years while tipping off the Ochrana in time to protect the lives of the high-ranking targets the party had chosen for assassination. Federoff could not understand the British system of law and what constituted being an accessory to a crime. He had been charged with conspiracy to commit murder:

What conspiracy? Simply because I knew him, that Fritz. And this is conspiracy. I don't understand. I will perhaps be charged for having known my father and mother. Awful, simply awful. The devil knows who he was: he did not carry a label on his nut. As an evidence the English authorities [court] will perhaps adopt the method of the devilish Azeff as an explanation for everything. The proceeding at the Police Court on Thursday put very much of this into one's mind.[31]

Regarding the connections between the British police, the terrorists and the Ochrana, Richard Deacon has speculated that the British secret service also had a hand in these affairs. He claims that Soviet sources later identified Peter the Painter as a counter-revolutionary operative named Serge Makharov alias Ivan Nikoliaieff, who had been assigned the task of spying on terrorists in the main cities of Europe. An impoverished aristocrat, Makharov was instructed to locate the revolutionaries in London and find some means of involving them in trouble with the British police with the object of creating a public demand for their expulsion from Britain.

As a result of the Russian counter-espionage activities in London to discredit the revolutionaries a curious new situation arose. The police, who were not told of these activities by the Secret Service, were generally hostile to all foreigners in the East End of London and came to look upon the Anarchists as criminals. The Secret Service on the other hand were generally sympathetic to the Anarchists and hostile to

*the Russian government agents, regarding the activities of the later as
an illegal intervention on British soil.*[32]

Deacon goes on to suggest that Winston Churchill's personal involvement in the Sidney Street siege was necessary because the entire operation against the Leesma organization involved delicate questions about
those strange *quid pro quo* arrangements in the field of secret service in
which governments undoubtedly engage. Churchill's presence was due
to the fact that as home secretary 'he knew all about the ramifications of
counter-espionage which this siege involved'.[33]

With the help of the Ochrana and the assistance of willing Judas
figures within the East End refugee community, together with the aid of
well over 1000 police and detectives 'turning over' the addresses
supplied to the authorities, the city police seemed to be well on the way
to unravelling the case. People were beginning to open up and information was beginning to flow when the Leesma terrorists struck once again
in an attempt to shut off police sources of intelligence amongst the
émigrés. On the night of 31 December 1910 they demonstrated the
extent of their influence to fellow immigrants with the brutal murder of
a Jew named Leon Beron on Clapham Common. That, at least, was the
effect created in the public mind by the murder, and the police were
disbelieved when they continued to insist that the corpse on Clapham
Common had no connection with the Houndsditch and Sidney Street
affairs. Leon Beron lived in Jubilee Street, Steinie Morrison, the man
alleged to have murdered him lived in Grove Street, and Beron's brother
stated that Leon had had business of a suspicious nature in Sidney Street
and informed the police that he intended to search every house in it to
find his brother's killer.[34] This, it must be remembered, was shortly
before the police precipitated the siege at 100 Sidney Street, and the
street had not yet become notorious.

There are other factors, which will be dealt with in the next chapter,
which help to demonstrate that the police were wrong and that there was
a direct connection between the Clapham Common murder and the
Leesma organization, but here it is sufficient to point out that the popular press never doubted it, nor did the defense attorney for Steinie
Morrison.

Leon Beron had been brutally battered to death with an iron bar. He
had been the victim of an almost inconceivably ferocious attack and had
received terrible multiple injuries to the head while the left ear hung
almost severed. After death, the corpse had been stabbed repeatedly in
the chest, and the face had been deliberately hacked into two symme-
trical gashes which looked like an elongated letter 'S'. These injuries
seemed to bear evidence of a hatred that even death could not expunge.
The press was fascinated by the details of this murder, and the
mysterious train of events that could lead to an apparently respectable
man wandering about Clapham Common at night in the middle of

winter. Even more intriguing, however, was the question of the significance of the facial marking.

Great importance obviously attaches, or may attach to these incisions
... The authorities think it quite likely that these marks are the sign
of a secret society, but they also point out that it is a common custom
among Slavonic races to mark with cuts of various kinds the faces,
generally the foreheads, of those killed by violence.[35]

At the coroner's inquest, Dr Joseph Needham, Divisional Surgeon of
Police, commented that the facial furrowing could not have been caused
accidentally nor would such incisions have been inflicted by persons
whose only intention was the taking of life. Needham drew attention to
the symmetry of the marks which was extraordinary, and confessed that
he was baffled to explain why a murderer should stay behind to inflict
such wounds. To the coroner's suggestion that the marks were some
sort of sign, Needham replied, 'I think so. There is a meaning in them.'
These findings were echoed by Dr Freyberger, who conducted the post
mortem on Beron.[36]

Nor did the uncertainty end there. The more that was revealed about
Leon Beron and his alleged murderer, Steinie Morrison, the greater the
mystery became. Concerning Beron, there were many unanswered
questions. He apparently lived a respectable life of ease. He did not work
and spent the whole of his days talking to the patrons of a nearby
tearoom and café. His income, derived from a few small, rented pro-
perties, was quite tiny, yet he was a man of substance who wore a gold
watch and heavy gold chain on which hung a five-guinea piece. This
watch and its accoutrements would have represented more than a year's
income for him.[37] Moreover, he and his two brothers were said to have
claims on a London estate of fabulous value, but that their rightful claims
were being thwarted by a firm of solicitors and they had come to England
in 1894 to protect their interests. They had apparently remained in
London, however, for sixteen years without making any attempt to
establish the validity of their alleged entitlement.

Steinie Morrison, similarly, conveyed the impression that he possessed
hidden depths. Well over 6-feet tall and a handsome 'ladies' man', he
used a number of aliases and at one time claimed to be a Russian named
Alexander Petropavloff, born in 1879 in Korsousk in the district of
Liutzin, government of Vitebsk, Russia. In court he claimed to have been
been born in Sydney, Australia, around 1882, and as a small boy to have
accompanied his mother when she returned to Russia where he lived
with her until he reached adulthood.

Following the siege of Sidney Street and Morrison's arrest a few days
later, because he had been seen in Beron's company by a number of eyewitnesses on the night of the killing, the newspapers were unable to resist
speculating on the connection between the crimes and wondering
whether Morrison or Beron had any links with the Lettish terrorists.

Meanwhile, in view of the coincidence that the dead man had associa-
tions with the alien quarter of the East End, the question has been
raised whether there is any connection between the Clapham and the
Houndsditch murders. Mrs Josephine, a sister of the dead man,
yesterday stated that she knew that he had had some dealings with a
man in Sidney Street, Stepney. She did not know the nature of the
business, but her younger brother she added seemed to connect Sidney
Street with the murder. [38]

Several days later, *The Times* dutifully reported that detectives
discredited the idea that there were any links between the crimes, or that
the mysterious marks carved into the dead man's face were of any
significance or indicated the operations of some secret society whose
hatred the dead man had incurred. This marked the beginning of a
cover-up. For their own purposes the police had propagated the view
-wrongly - that politics played no part in the Houndsditch murders. The
question is did they do the same thing with the Clapham Common
Crime? After all, the evidence of the police surgeon before the coroner's
court had been responsible for giving substance to rumours concerning
the 'S' shaped incisions on Beron's face. *The Times* repeated the police
orthodoxy, but two days later added an illuminating account of the
extraordinary interest shown in these marks by newspapers on the
continent. The paper's correspondent in Vienna reported:

The details of the murder of the man Beron have aroused no less
interest here than the Sidney Street affair, and many conjectures are
made as to the meaning of the cuts resembling the letter 'S' on the
face of the victim. The most interesting suggestion is made by a Vien-
nese expert in criminal investigation who informs the News Wiener
Tagblatt *that several cases of disfigurement by similar signs are*
recorded by the police. This kind of disfigurement is known among the
criminal classes as slichener, *that is 'traitor' signs. The initial letter of*
the word slichener *is usually cut out with a knife on the face of the*
supposed traitor ... The cuts on the face of Beron were doubtless
meant to indicate that he had been killed as a traitor. Professor Hans
Gross, of Graz, who is regarded as an authority in criminal lore, states
to the Tagblatt *that the marks on the face of Beron may quite as well*
be the Hebrew character Schihn *as the Latin 'S'. It would mean that*
the victim was to be marked by some word of the criminal jargon
beginning with 'sch' for instance Schlosser, *the equivalent for*
policeman or police spy. [39]

The Houndsditch and Clapham crimes intersected in one other way. The
men and women arrested for complicity in the Houndsditch murders
were kept under close observation the whole time they were in prison
awaiting trial. Every move they made, every letter they wrote, every

scrap of conversation that might help the police, was reported quickly by the prison authorities. On 28 January 1911, Warder T. Russel reported to Brixton Prison's deputy medical officer 'As Prisoner - S. Morrison -was leaving the Hospital for discharge this morning, Prisoner Y. Dubof came towards him and remarked "Wish you success." How well did these two know one another? Was Morrison also part of the anti-tsarist underground in London? Had Beron really been killed as a warning, or in reprisal for giving information to the police? Was Beron's death the reason for the extraordinary lengths to which the police went to avoid using the name of their secret informer? Other informants' names are scattered through the records, why then the reticence in this case if not to protect an important agent from similar retribution by the Lettish terrorists and their friends? The Russian consul general recognized the danger, hence his insistence that police interview the spy only in his presence and in the anonymity of railway-station or public house.

The murder of Leon Beron certainly slowed police progress in solving the Leesma crimes, but arrests continued to be made as the authorities rounded up the members of group 5. Eventually, the only two missing were the successful escapees Peter Piaktow and the experienced sneak-thief Max Smoller, both of whom had got out of England and away to the continent. Jacob Fogel, 'Bifsteks', and other members of the Leesma organization were not arrested, although the police had their names plus several others supplied by Charles Perelman. Evidence connecting them directly with the crime was hard to find, and British law did not permit the arrest of a suspected criminal's friends. In this case the cellular structure of the Leesma organization probably protected its members from arrest on conspiracy charges, and Peter Piaktow's and Fritz's effectiveness as *agents provocateurs* was restricted to the single cell.

With the tacit consent of the authorities, Gardstein, Svaars, and Sokolow, the three dead terrorists, became scapegoats for the rest of the group, and the police made this much easier by bungling the ballistics information and blaming George Gardstein for the killings rather than the real culprit, Jacob Peters. The other members of the group quickly followed suit and informed their captors that Fritz Svaars and William Sokolow were the other two men present at the murders of Bentley, Choat and Tucker. The authorities were already predisposed towards this tidy solution and accepted the story quite readily, thereby enabling the hapless Svaars and Sokolow to become far more useful to the gang dead than they could ever have been alive. The obduracy and desperation of their last stand at Sidney Street inclined the police to the opinion that the same men had been equally as ferocious that December night at Exchange Buildings in Houndsditch. Why should they have fought with such frenzied courage if they were not guilty of the earlier crime? Jacob Peters had begun to blame Fritz from the moment he was arrested. His first words, when confronted by the squad of detectives sent to appre-hend him, were 'I am not responsible for what my cousin Fritz has done.' At this time, Fritz was still very much alive, and Peters was obviously prepared to save his own skin at the expense of his cousin's.[40]

When Nina Vassileva was arrested, she told the authorities that Gardstein, Svaars, Sokolow and Max Smoller were the men involved in the Houndsditch killings, and that Smoller had deliberately shot Gardstein because he wanted to be the leader of the group. Nina, it should be remembered, had been George Gardstein's lover, and she had no doubts just who had 'accidentally' shot him in the back during the fracas with the police. She gave them Smoller's name but otherwise followed the orthodox policy of making scapegoats of the dead men.[41]

This *modus operandi* was made much easier for the arrested members of group 5 by the presiding judge at their trial. Mr Justice Grantham was, to put it bluntly, a bungler on the bench. Not only did he earn a public rebuke from Asquith, the Liberal Prime Minister of the day, for making an overtly political speech in favour of the Tories[42] but his decisions tended, more often than not, to be overturned in the court of appeal.[43] Early in the trial of the Leesma members, Grantham amazed the court by stating his personal conviction that the three men who were clearly the murderers had already met their doom, and he named George Gardstein, Fritz Svaars and William Sokolow as the three killers. He went on to rule that charges of conspiracy to commit murder could not be preferred against the rest of Leesma cell 5, and the prosecution was forced to reduce the charges to conspiracy to break and enter, and even here there was insufficient evidence to obtain a conviction. The defense attorneys resolutely followed the line that only four or five conspirators had been involved, these being the three dead scapegoats plus Max Smoller and Peter Piaktow. Luba Milstein repudiated her earlier statement to the police and now swore that Fritz Svaars, William Sokolow and Max Smoller had carried the wounded George Gardstein into Peter the Painter's room at 59 Grove Street. Karl Hoffman, her new protector, backed up this story. Yourka Dubof, Jacob Peters and John Rosen all claimed that they had been mere acquaintances of Fritz's and it was coincidental that they had all been together at Grove Street on the eve of the shootings.

Jacob Peters and Osip Federoff were provided with a lawyer by the Social Democratic Party, and the Russian consulate ensured that the others were provided with legal representation. The one notable exception was Nina Vassileva who was abandoned by the rest of the group. It seems likely that Nina had been only a fringe member of the Leesma organization involved solely because of her affair with Gardstein, and the others appear to have made a conscious decision to offer her up as a sacrifice to the English judicial system. The police had a stronger case against Nina Vassileva than against any of the others because they had found a bottle in a cupboard at number 11 Exchange Buildings in Houndsditch which bore her fingerprints, whilst no such damning evidence had turned up to incriminate anyone else. Whatever the reason, she was left undefended and alone until the philosophical anarchist Rudolf Rocker sent his wife to visit her in prison. The Rockers quickly provided Nina Vassileva with legal representation.[44] In the event, the prosecution failed miserably and all the others got off scot-free. Nina, however, was found guilty and sentenced to two years' imprisonment. In typical form, Mr Justice Grantham misdirected the jury, and five weeks later Nina Vassileva's sentence was quashed by the court of appeal and she too was set free.

Mr Justice Grantham's involvement in the case did not end there. Apparently the judge was an indefatigable souvenir hunter, and once the formalities of the trial had been completed, he wrote to the commissioner of police requesting that he be given as a keepsake one of the mauser pistols found in the wreckage of Sidney Street. He concluded this letter with the curious comment that he felt 'the trial ended quite as well as we could have expected'.[45] Since Nina had been the only member of the organization convicted, and because nobody believed she had actually been anything more than an onlooker at the shootings, it is difficult to understand what the judge meant by his remark. The prosecution believed quite firmly that the other men had been accessories to murder, and it is hard to conceive that the police would have shared Mr Justice Grantham's conviction that the trial had ended as well as could have been expected.

During the trial Mr Grantham commented that in his view, on the evidence presented, Peter the Painter could not be prosecuted successfully for conspiracy to murder or even conspiracy to break and enter Harris's jewellery shop. There was no evidence that Peter had been connected in any way with the shootings. However, the police had published a reward poster and offered £500 for information leading to his arrest. In the public mind Peter the Painter was already larger than life. His evasion of arrest and his presumed escape overseas despite the massive manhunt organized by the police, is consonant with the view that he was an artful professional *agent provocateur* who could vanish at will into well-prepared bolt-holes. Peter went direct to Pavel Molchanoff's room as soon as it became obvious that escape was necessary. From there he vanished. It is significant that when Charles Perelman visited Fritz Svaars and William Sokolow in hiding at 100 Sidney Street after the shootings, the address Fritz wanted him to find was that of a man named Pavel. They seemed to know that the name had some connection with escape, but they had no idea of where he lived nor how to contact him. Peter, on the other hand, went straight to him, woke him at 2 am, and disappeared forever by mid-afternoon the same day.[46] It is obvious that he knew exactly where to go and what to do.

The authorities themselves agreed with Mr Justice Grantham that they did not have sufficient evidence on which to convict Peter. In 1913, the chief of police in Winnipeg, Canada wrote that he had positive information that Peter the Painter lived in the city and that he would be pleased to act in conjunction with the British police if they desired his apprehension. The result was a reply which reluctantly acknowledged that in this at least the judge had been correct.

The above named man was an associate of the persons who committed the Houndsditch Murders. He was living with one of them and was himself suspected of being concerned in the crime, but no conclusive proof was obtained that he was actually concerned; it is therefore not desirable that he should be arrested in connection with the matter if he is found abroad as there is not sufficient evidence to justify application for his extradition.[47]

In 1911 a similar reply had been sent to the commissioner of police in Perth, Western Australia;[48] and in 1917 the same response was made to a further application from Melbourne, Australia.

The City of London police refused to admit publicly that they were no longer anxious to obtain the arrest of Peter Piaktow, but on every occasion when a suspect could have been arrested overseas, either in Europe or further abroad, they were forced to acknowledge that they possessed insufficient evidence to warrant the implementation of extradition proceedings. Did the London police fail to make a public statement of the fact that they were no longer interested in Peter the Painter to avoid further ridicule and loss of face? Or was it perhaps part of a conscious policy of disclosing as little as possible to their potential enemies amongst the anti-tsarist terrorists? Whatever the reasons, the failure of the British authorities to make such an open, unequivocal statement had immediate repercussions and may well have been directly responsible for events in Australia which a future Prime Minister, John Curtin, was later to describe as 'a monstrous proceeding'.[49] The debacles at Houndsditch and Sidney Street were destined to have a profound effect on the lives of other Lettish refugees, including at least one member of the Leesma terrorist organization who had been more fortunate than Fritz Svaars and had actually made good an escape to the country of his dreams, 'the blessed land of Australia'.

FOOTNOTES

1 *The Times*, 19 December 1910.
2 Donald Rumbelow, op. cit., pp. 142-52.
3 Houndsditch Papers.
4 ibid.
5 ibid.

6   ibid.
7   ibid.
8   ibid.
9   ibid.
10 ibid.
11 ibid.
12 ibid.
13 ibid.
14 ibid.
15 *The Times*, 5 January 1911.
16 Houndsditch Papers.
17 ibid.
18 ibid.
19 ibid.
20 ibid.
21 ibid.
22 ibid.
23 *The Times*, 8 February 1911.
24 Houndsditch Papers.
25 ibid.
26 ibid.
27 ibid.
28 Ronald Hingley, op. cit., p. 76.
29 Houndsditch Papers.
30 Donald Rumbelow, op. cit., p. 48
31 Houndsditch Papers.
32 Richard Deacon, *A History of the British Secret Service*, London, 1969, pp. 131-2.
33 ibid.
34 *The Times*, 4 January 1911.
35 ibid., 6 January 1911.
36 ibid.
37 H. Fletcher Moulton (ed.), 'The Trial of Steinie Morrison', *Notable British Trials*, Edinburgh, 1922, p. xxi.
38 *The Times*, 4 January 1911.
39 *The Times*, 9 January 1911.
40 Houndsditch Papers.
41 ibid.
42 *Hansard's Parliamentary Debates*, 5th series, vol. 21, 1911, col. 291.
43 *The Times*, 9 February 1911.
44 Houndsditch Papers.
45 ibid.
46 ibid.
47 ibid.
48 See next chapter.
49 Western Australian Police Department file 3911/1911.

4
'THE
BLESSED
LAND
OF
AUSTRALIA'

The focus of attention now shifts to Western Australia and involves several members of the Leesma organization who had been part of group 5. The foremost of these was the lodger nicknamed 'Yahnit', who had been mentioned by the informer Theodore Jansen as an associate of Jansen's other lodger, Karl Hoffman. Jansen's statements to the police had described Yahnit as a Lett who evinced extraordinary interest in the Houndsditch murders and the affray at Sidney Street. Indeed, when the police came to arrest Karl Hoffman, Jansen informed them that the man they ought really to have been interested in had fled. When the police swooped on Hoffman, Yahnit, who used the names of August Maren or Peter Jansen, was already en route to Western Australia. He was not destined, however, to escape entirely the consequences of his membership of the Leesma group.

How did an anti-tsarist revolutionary from the Baltic provinces become an emigrant to Western Australia? It began with a Lettish sailor named Ernest Dreger who innocently blundered into a situation that was to test him to the limits of his endurance. Dreger had been born in Riga in 1881 and had gone to sea when he was twenty. In 1907 he jumped ship in Western Australia and worked for nearly a year as a farm labourer clearing land in the district of Kellerberrin. Towards the end of 1908 he left Western Australia and worked as a fireman shovelling coal aboard a German freighter. After being paid off in Rotterdam, Dreger crossed to London, arriving there in June or July 1909. He became ill and entered the Seaman's Hospital in London. Whilst in hospital, he made the acquaintance of a fellow Lettish sailor named Peter Jansen or 'Yahnit', whom he was later to know as August Maren. Upon his discharge from hospital, Dreger moved to the Scandinavian Sailors' Home and once more found his new friend Yahnit there. The two men became quite close, and when Dreger returned to the Home, following his next voyage to South Africa, he found a letter waiting for him from his friend informing him that Yahnit had found private accommodation as a lodger with a family named Ligum. The Ligums also came from Lettland, as did their other lodger, a man introduced to Dreger as George Rosenberg, but whom he was later to know as Fred Johnson. Johnson intimated to Dreger that he was Mrs Esther Ligum's lover and that she had kept him for the past two years. Mrs Ligum also had a seventeen-year-old daughter named Sarah, in whom the three men were interested, but Johnson was committed to the girl's mother, whilst Maren and Dreger managed to suppress any jealousies and took the girl on outings with them when Dreger visited the house three or four times a week.

Ernest Dreger left on another voyage, and while he was away Mrs Ligum and her lodgers moved to another house in Back Church Lane off Ellen Street, a district described by *The Times* as one of the very worst in London's East End.[1] When he returned to London, Dreger took lodgings with Mrs Ligum and renewed his relationship with Maren and the girl. Sarah evidently found the attentions of the experienced sailor flattering, and she and Dreger came to an agreement that he would return to Australia and establish himself and then send for her to come out and marry him. Maren at this stage did not contest the suit between Dreger and the girl, and indeed arranged that Dreger would also send him a ticket for Australia from the proceeds of his work. Mrs Ligum saw Dreger's departure as an opportunity to divest herself of Fred Johnson, and Dreger was persuaded to smuggle him aboard his ship. When the S S *Port Chalmers* had been several days at sea, Johnson emerged from the coal bunker in which he had been hiding and was permitted to work his passage to Australia. He left the ship at Albany in Western Australia, while Ernest Dreger continued on to Adelaide in South Australia, where he also left the ship. From Adelaide Dreger travelled by land to Port Pirie.

There is an oral tradition within the Latvian community in Australia that in the early years of the twentieth century before the First World War, some form of underground organization existed at Port Pirie. It was an illegal operation that actively encouraged Lettish sailors to desert their ships, and it provided safe hiding places for such illegal immigrants together with sufficient funds to enable them to move to other parts of Australia and submerge themselves in the wider population. No records can be found of its activities, which is not really surprising, but its existence might explain why Fritz Svaars had been determined to come to Australia, and why Ernest Dreger travelled to Port Pirie after leaving his ship in Adelaide.[2]

At Port Pirie Dreger joined another Lettish sailor named Peter Older, and the two men travelled together to Western Australia in August 1910. They went to the Kellerberrin district, with which Dreger was already familiar, and took work as farm labourers. Within a month Ernest Dreger went to Perth, the capital city of Western Australia, and sent four tickets for third-class passenger travel to Western Australia back to London. The tickets were for Maren, Dreger's two brothers Adolf and William – still living in Riga – and for young Sarah Ligum. Maren's ticket was purchased in his new name as he requested, and since

Lettish refugees seemed to change names at will, such a request would probably not then have appeared so odd as it would now. What is inexplicable is just how Ernest Dreger could afford this expenditure within a month of his return to Western Australia. It does not seem possible for him to have earned the sum required, even though the newcomers would be sailing as nominated immigrants, which meant effectively that the commonwealth and the Western Australian state government subsidized the fares and approved the four as immigrants.

The whole question is clouded by the fact that immigration was one of the areas of jurisdiction passed to the commonwealth government by the Australian states at federation. It had not really been much of a surrender, however, as it was not practical for the commonwealth to take over immediate responsibility in 1901, and the transmission of effective administrative power from the states to the commonwealth was a gradual one. Professor A.T. Yarwood shows that although in 1901 the new federal government had been vested with power to make laws on immigration and emigration for the whole nation, the earlier colonial legislation in these areas remained on the statute books. Also, because the various states in the new federation already possessed experienced officers who administered their immigration laws, it was thought to be unnecessary for the commonwealth to create a separate staff of its own, and the state officials administered the commonwealth's legislation in addition to that already enacted by the state governments.[3] Nor were the federal authorities keen to take over full responsibility for immigration. The states provided substantial funds each year to subsidize immigration, and the commonwealth was anxious not to jeopardize these funds by a course of action which would leave it to bear the entire financial burden of assisted immigration. At a special conference held in Melbourne in 1908 and attended by Prime Minister Alfred Deakin, it was resolved that the federal authorities should co-operate with the states in promoting and otherwise assisting immigration to Australia by a general advertising campaign in Britain, designed to highlight the advantages Australia offered to immigrants; but that all matters relating to the selection of individual immigrants be left in the hands of the several states.[4] This system was reviewed in 1914 and attention was drawn to the fact that the states were likely to reduce their financial commitment to immigration if the commonwealth became too intrusive. A measure of the respective levels of financial contribution from the states and the federal authorities can be gained from the realization that between 1911 and 1913 the commonwealth government spent £40,000 in advertising, and the states expended altogether about £650,000 in contributions towards immigrants' passages and fees to immigration agents. The commonwealth's position paper makes the cogent comment:

A direct connection of immigration with the land naturally has influenced the States at various conferences to express an opinion

against allowing the Commonwealth to take complete control of immi-
gration. In any event, if we did so, the Commonwealth expenditure
would probably be three-quarters of a million a year. Taking the
political as well as the economic relations of the expenditure into
account, any change proposed or assented to by the Commonwealth
should not go beyond subsidizing in cash the efforts of the States . . .
The method of apportionment among the States must have regard to
the probability that the States if not checked will correspondingly
reduce their outlay.[5]

Thus, when Ernest Dreger decided to bring out his fiancée as well as his
brothers and his friend, he was able to tap Western Australian government funds to subsidize their passages. He brought out his fellow Letts
under a local scheme known as the Nominated System of Immigration.
In the first decade after federation most of the Australian states offered
two methods of assistance to would-be immigrants.[6] Firstly, they
subsidized the passages to Australia of immigrants and their families who
had been inspected and selected as suitable by salaried immigration
agents in London. The second form of subsidy catered for those immigrants who had been nominated as suitable by someone already resident
in one of the states. The Western Australian representative to the 1908
conference summarized the state government's views on the sort of
immigrants Western Australia desired. It was all very well for a state like
Victoria which gave promise of becoming a large manufacturing and
industrial centre to favour artisans of different sorts, but Western
Australia wanted none who were not prepared to go on the land. To
obtain assisted passages, such immigrants had to possess capital to the
value of £50, and the state's agent general in London had been instructed
that it was essential for such migrants to possess some knowledge of
agriculture. People who satisfied these criteria had half the cost of their
passages paid by the state government. Obviously, Ernest Dreger's
nominees could not qualify for assistance under this scheme, but there
was also a variant of the subsidy described to the conference, and it was
this alternative scheme that was used by Dreger. It was known as the
Nominated System, and enabled persons resident in Western Australia,
or Western Australians temporarily resident in Britain, to nominate
people desiring to migrate to the state at a cost which fluctuated between
£6 and £15.10. No money qualification was required in the case of
nominated immigrants, but the nominator had to undertake to look after
the immigrants on their arrival, and to ensure that they did not become a
charge upon the state.[7]
   On 20 September 1910, Ernest Dreger nominated Maren, his two
brothers and his proposed wife as immigrants to Western Australia. At
the minimum rate possible, this would have cost him at least £24. Where
did the money come from? One possibility is that Dreger collected it
from the Lettish group in Port Pirie who might well have provided some

funds for bringing out fellow countrymen. Perhaps Dreger earned the money. He must have been paid for the voyage from London to Adelaide, and it may have been that he only needed to work for a month to earn sufficient to cover the costs of his nominations. He might also have been given money from Leesma expropriations in London in order to provide sanctuary for Maren in Australia. The source of the money remains a mystery, but it is a weakness in Ernest Dreger's explanation of events that he never accounted for it.

In the meantime, Dreger and Peter Older had been joined at Kellerberrin by Fred Johnson, and the three men worked clearing scrub together while they waited to be reunited with their friends.

In London during these intervening months, events were moving rapidly towards the climax of Houndsditch and Sidney Street. The three months before Christmas were a busy time for the Leesma expropriators in cell 5 as they finalized their plans for the raid on Harris's jewellery store. In personal matters, also, these months proved a trying time for all concerned. As Ernest Dreger's absence from England lengthened from weeks to months, Sarah Ligum began to pay attention to August Maren who possessed the inestimable advantage of being close at hand. She was, after all, a very young girl and her fiancée was thousands of miles away. Her mother became quite concerned over her daughter's growing involvement with a non-Jewish man – she had never approved of Ernest Dreger either – and she begged her new lover, an orthodox Jew named Louis Hersberg, to speak to Sarah in an attempt to break up the relationship between Maren and the girl. When Dreger's tickets plus £8 in cash arrived from Western Australia, Mrs Ligum also requested Hersberg to try and dissuade the girl from leaving. At the same time she refused to allow Maren to remain as a lodger in her house 'because he was too familiar with my daughter Sarah'.[8] Hersberg's intervention took the form of a lecture to the girl on the moral dangers incurred by young Jewish girls who associated with non-Jewish men. It was a genuine and apparently well meant attempt to please Sarah's mother, but it so enraged Maren that he threatened to kill Hersberg for his interference. When the frightened Jew advised Mrs Ligum to go to the police, Maren again threatened to kill him. This quarrel occurred during December 1910 and January 1911, at a time when the entire East End of London was agog with the events at Houndsditch and Sidney Street, and with the Clapham Common killing. Maren moved out of the Ligum house and Theodore Jansen reported to the police that he had a temporary lodger during this time named 'Yahnit'. Jansen permitted his lodgers to use his name for mail, and it should be remembered that at this time in London Maren was known as Peter Jansen or 'Yahnit', while Karl Hoffman had used the name Lonnie Jansen (the name of Jansen's wife) for his mail deliveries.

Maren, Sarah Ligum and Ernest Dreger's two brothers were booked to leave London for Western Australia on 3 February 1911 aboard the

RMS *Otway*. Adolf and William Dreger arrived in London from Riga on 2 February 1911 and travelled straight to Mrs Ligum's boarding house. What they made of the strained atmosphere there can only be guessed at, but Sarah and her mother took them to visit Maren in a room at 22 Tarling Street nearby, and the next day all four embarked for Australia. The previous evening, however, they had all visited some of Maren's friends to say goodbye, and when they were returning Maren had informed them that he was wanted by the police; he betrayed extreme nervousness when they were walking in the open street.[9] Since this was shortly after the siege at Sidney Street and before the arrest of Karl Hoffman, and the streets of the East End were full of plain-clothes policemen and potential informers, members of the Leesma organization like Maren could be excused for feeling rather like hunted animals.

The ship sailed just three days before the London police swooped on Hoffman, and Maren's sense of relief at his escape can be gauged from the statement made by Adolf Dreger and confirmed by Sarah Ligum, that as his distance from Britain increased he became increasingly expansive and boastful.[10] After the ship had left Port Said in Egypt, Maren began to swagger in an apparent attempt to impress Adolf and William and to raise his stature in the eyes of the eighteen-year-old Sarah. He informed Adolf that he was a member of an association of Russians who had planned to rob a 'gold magazine' in London in order to finance and support their friends in Russia. Maren claimed to be one of the leaders of this group. He had taken Sarah Ligum to the Jubilee Street club on many occasions, and also at least once to the Social Democratic Club in Charlotte Street with Ernest Dreger. On this occasion Maren had delivered a public address which had been so well received that he was judged to be the best speaker of the evening and had been requested to address the meeting again before it ended. The association referred to by Maren seems to have been the Leesma organization; he told Adolf Dreger that four or five of their best men had been chosen to rob Harris's jewellery shop, and that while they were there, they had been interrupted by the police and started fighting. One of their men had been hurt and had been carried to one of their 'mates's houses' where he had died. He added that the other men ran away and that two of them went to a house where the association stored its fighting and burglary instruments and stayed there until a fight with the soldiers broke out.[11] Maren possibly provided an explanation of the seemingly inexhaustible ammunition supply used by Fritz Svaars and William Sokolow during the seven or so hours of the Sidney Street siege. If Betsy Gershon had been quarter-master for all the Leesma stores, there would have been no shortage of ammunition, and eyewitnesses had commented on the prodigality with which the two men had maintained their automatic weapons fire. To this point, also, Maren's story fits the account given to police by Charles Perelman, the Ochrana agent, who insisted that Betsy Gershon had been hiding the two wanted men since they first went to ground on the Saturday following the Houndsditch killings. This was never publicized in the press, and the public was told that Fritz and William had forced Mrs Gershon to hide them only one day before the siege. Maren, therefore, did seem to know what he was talking about.

Sarah Ligum's statement directs attention to yet another incident that indicates a link between August Maren and the Leesma group. She mentions that on the night after the Houndsditch murders she was taken by Maren to a room in Tarling Street where she met a woman whose name she did not know, but whose nickname was 'Quickmate'. This woman claimed to have visited Grove Street to see Fritz Svaars and that, when she opened the door, she found the police lying in wait. They took her for interrogation before letting her go. 'Maren spoke to her, and asked her how she knew about it, but she would not say much because I was there.'[12] Once again, this account squares with the known facts. Svaars was participating in an amateur theatrical production being planned for the Jubilee Street Club's Christmas show. Ironically, he had been cast in the role of a police officer. The London police recognized 'Quickmate' from Sarah Ligum's statement as probably being a girl named Ougusta Grand whom they had arrested briefly when she called to find out why Fritz failed to attend rehearsals.[13] Most London newspapers had carried this story as a release from the Associated Press Agency.

The story was told yesterday of the appearance of Fritz, one of the men wanted in connection with the crime in the role of actor, and of his rehearsing the part of a police officer in a Russian Socialist play to be performed in Spitalfields on Boxing Night. Yesterday a press representative obtained an interview with another member of the cast, a young Russian woman, named Ougusta Grand, of Nelson Street, Commercial Road, who said, in her broken English, 'I only see Fritz two times.' She went on to say: ' He was brought into the sketch by Mr Grube, and was very nice in every way. He did not say much about himself. He told me he was a single man. He used to play on the Mandoline, but not very well. I was the only woman in the play, and I took the part of the boy who was shot. We have rehearsed the piece two times together, and were to have another practice on Saturday afternoon. As Fritz did not turn up, I went to the place where he was staying, at 59 Grove Street. When I got there the police stopped me, and took me to the police station. I was very frightened, for I knew nothing of what was the matter, and I could only tell the police what I have told you. I was allowed to go home at 3 o'clock on Sunday. I do not know any more about Fritz, nor do I know any of his friends.[14]

Ernest Dreger's later statement from gaol to the police in Western Australia similarly shed more light on Maren's London activities.

Dreger remembered the speech Maren had given to the Social Democrats and also that Fred Johnson had been a regular attender at the Social
Democrat meetings. Johnson was reputed to be wanted by the Russian
authorities for several murders committed near Riga during the 1905
Revolution. Maren had also boasted to Ernest Dreger of his involvement
with the group of men who had planned the Houndsditch robbery and
fought the army at Sidney Street. It is in his account of his own
antecedents, however, that Maren provided useful information to Dreger
which can be cross-checked against Maren's own statement to the police.
Both accounts claim that August Maren had been a schoolteacher in
Russia, that he had experienced difficulties because he was an anti-tsarist
activist and had spent some time in gaol for his beliefs. Dreger claimed
Maren was an anarchist, while Maren himself proclaimed that he was a
Social Democrat. Although such distinctions were important to their
contemporaries in the anti-tsarist movement, it was an unimportant
distinction where the Leesma group was concerned. Besides, the correspondence left by George Gardstein makes it clear that anarchist
terrorists found it easier to masquerade as respectable Social Democrats
than to operate openly in Europe.[15] Maren certainly possessed sufficient
credibility as a Social Democrat to claim the acquaintance of the famous
Swedish socialist Hjalmer Branting. It had been Branting who
established the tradition of assisting Russian opponents of tsarism in
Sweden, and he became one of the exiled Lenin's trusted advisers.
Branting himself was later to become three times prime minister of
Sweden.[16] Maren claimed that the influential Branting had befriended
him in Sweden in 1909, and had given him letters of introduction to
other revolutionaries.[17] Ernest Dreger stated that Maren had bragged of
his importance in the anarchist movement and had stressed his
conviction that he and the Dregers should work in Australia the way
Peter the Painter and his friends did in London, and that one day they
might see Peter himself in Australia. Finally, Dreger announced that
Maren intended bringing some of his anarchist comrades to Australia,
including a Lettish couple named Jansen from London. This seems most
likely to have been Theodore and Lonnie Jansen, the landlord of Karl
Hoffman and Maren, and would-be police informer.

Finally, and most conclusively, the Western Australia police sent
photographs of Maren to London where they were shown to the 'certain
person' who betrayed Fritz Svaars and William Sokolow. Perelman
immediately recognized Maren as a close personal friend of Peter
Piaktow's and as a man who had fled England shortly after the
Houndsditch murders. He informed the London police that August
Maren had been connected with the murders and that he believed Peter
the Painter could be traced through him.[18]

August Maren's story, as recounted in the statements of the Dregers
and Sarah Ligum, has been shown to be consonant with the known facts
of the Houndsditch and Sidney Street affairs and with what has come to

light concerning the organization behind these incidents. Maren was not only identified by Charles Perelman as a close personal friend of Peter the Painter's and as a member of the Leesma group, but he also appeared in one of the photographs police confiscated from Sara Trassjonsky when she was arrested. The photograph was of three unidentified men, and August Maren is clearly the man on the right of the trio. Maren's involvement with the Leesma organization is beyond doubt.

Another aspect of Maren's activities with the Leesma group causes some difficulty, for August Maren claimed that the murder of Leon Beron on Clapham Common had also been a Leesma operation undertaken in a conscious attempt to spread fear amongst the Jewish inhabitants of London's East End, and to bring home to them the sort of reprisals they could expect if they passed on to the police information about the Lettish revolutionaries. According to the Dregers, Maren boasted of his role in this killing and explained that Leon Beron had not been killed because he was an informer but because he was regarded by the Leesma people as a potential informer.

A Jew wanted to tell the police about the Anarchists' movements and we found out what he was going to do. We got him one day in a paddock and we killed him. We cut his ears and nose and put Freemason's traitor marks on his face and then cut his throat. We did this to frighten the other Jews so as they would be afraid to tell where the Anarchists, who were wanted, were hiding.[19]

Maren's disclosure to Ernest Dreger at last provides the link between the two crimes of Houndsditch and Clapham Common that so baffled contemporaries and has remained a stumbling block to modern writers who sense the connection but cannot prove it.[20] Donald Rumbelow dismisses the view that the two crimes were connected for the same reasons that the jury at Steinie Morrison's trial rejected his lawyer's claim of a connection, namely that Leon Beron was not one of the men known to be a police informer during the investigation into the Houndsditch crime. Beron's name does not appear in police records among the long list of individuals from the East End who made voluntary or involuntary statements, and it appeared that the crimes had only a geographical nexus. However, Leon Beron was not killed as a punishment for informing. Maren's revelations to the Dregers illustrate that for Leesma personnel the killing was a pre-emptive operation, not a retaliatory one. Beron was murdered because somehow it had become known that he was contemplating betraying the Leesma organization to the police, and it was thought that such a violent death would be a warning to the entire Jewish community about the fate of traitors. Hence the ritualistic 'Freemasons' traitor marks' carved into the face of the dead man; the elongated letter 'S' was a common form of shorthand amongst the Leesma people to designate a Jew.[21] Rumbelow dismisses the notion that Beron had been murdered because he was an informer because the group had refrained from exterminating Nicolai Tomacoff who earned notoriety throughout the East End as a known police spy, and who must have been recognized as such by those Leesma members who were still at liberty. Tomacoff was not killed, therefore Beron could not have been murdered by the Leesma organization.[22] Such a view, however, tends to beg the question. Nicolai Tomacoff was accompanied by a policeman in his travels throughout London because he had provided information resulting in the arrests of Osip Federoff and Jacob Peters. He had been picked up by the police the day after the Houndsditch murders and had been assisting them ever since. A Leesma attempt on his life would have constituted an enormous provocation to the police and would have been counter-productive. Moreover, Tomacoff knew only the people in cell 5 and had already imparted to the police the little that he knew; after the first few days Tomacoff ceased to be a threat to the Leesma survivors.

The pre-emptive operation in Clapham Common was effective. It has already been noted that August Maren had twice threatened the life of the Jew Louis Hersberg if he involved the authorities in Maren's affairs. Yet despite this, when the police did approach Hersberg and request his assistance, the Jew's fear of reprisals led him to make the extraordinary claim that he had always believed Maren and his friends to have been 'respectable'.[23] Similarly, Sarah Ligum's mother Esther informed the police that, although she knew that Maren often took her daughter to a club in Jubilee Street, she had not been aware that it was an anarchist club, but had thought that it was only a place for dancing.[24] Since the club had been established by Rudolf Rocker, the editor of *Arbiter Fraint* (the Worker's Friend) the Jewish anarchist newspaper, and since there had been recurrent bouts of fisticuffs between Jewish anarchists and orthodox Jews in the streets outside the club and near the synagogue, such naivety does not carry conviction. It seems more likely that a worldly wise Esther Ligum was protecting herself against possible reprisals from the anti-tsarist groups still operating out of London. Back Church Lane, where she lived, was regarded as one of the most dangerous areas in London's East End, and it is not surprising to find both Esther and Hersberg demonstrating such artless simplicity when the police finally did solicit assistance from them.

August Maren slipped away from Mrs Ligum's house after the Clapham Common crime in which he had been involved personally. He stayed in the country for a short time, and when he returned to London, he lodged temporarily with several of his friends until the time came for his departure for Australia. Sarah Ligum visited him at these houses, and their romantic relationship apparently did not begin to cool until Ernest Dreger's two brothers arrived from Riga and the four assembled in London for the trip to Western Australia. The passenger list for the RMS *Otway* shows that Sarah posed as the wife of Adolf Dreger for the voyage, and Maren had little opportunity to renew his suit.[25] When the ship arrived at Fremantle on 7 March 1911, Ernest Dreger was there to meet them and immediately took charge of the girl. Maren said nothing.[26]

The four immigrants travelled with Ernest to his camp at Kellerberrin where they joined the other Letts, Fred Johnson and Peter Older. Ernest Dreger provided a tent for himself and Sarah, where they lived as man and wife. His brothers shared a second tent, and August Maren camped with Johnson and Older. Inevitable difficulties soon began to surface caused by Sarah's presence among six healthy young men. After the first few weeks the camp split into warring factions, with the Dregers on one side and Maren, Johnson and Older on the other. Maren had already threatened to kill one man in England for attempting to come between him and Sarah, and he greatly resented Ernest Dreger's proprietal attitude towards her. He complained to Adolf Dreger that he had more right to Sarah than Ernest, because he had had a longer relationship with her. Fred Johnson also became embroiled in the affair when he asserted that he too had a right to Sarah's favours, since he had lived with her and her mother in England.[27] Ernest Dreger successfully withstood these attempts to take the girl away from him and challenged the two men to fight him if they dared. He was a mature and strong man, a widely travelled sailor in peak physical condition after a season of hard rural labour in Western Australia, and wisely both Maren and Johnson declined his offer.

Once this disagreement had surfaced, however, life in the camp deteriorated rapidly. Dreger called Maren and Johnson 'Russian anarchist brutes' and forbade Sarah Ligum to speak to either of them. For her part, Sarah seemed to do little to calm things. She continued to speak to Maren and Johnson whenever she chose, and on one occasion when Ernest Dreger was away from the camp, she spent several hours privately in the tent with Fred Johnson. The men had been employed by a local farmer named Prowse, and he provided a measure of the degree to which the quality of life in the camp had declined when he informed the local police that he regarded all the Letts as dangerous men, that they appeared always to be feuding, and that they were continually chasing one another about with knives.

It was jealousy over Sarah Ligum that finally destroyed the friendship between Ernest Dreger and August Maren. Dreger had come to the conclusion that conditions were too unpleasant to continue life in the camp. Accordingly, late in March he travelled to the town of Northam to look for work on behalf of his two brothers. Adolf Dreger was a hairdresser, and employment in such a trade was only to be found in the towns. He travelled by train to Northam and met two men carrying swags and armed with a rifle and a double-barrelled shot-gun. Dreger asked whether they wished to sell the rifle as he wanted it to shoot kangaroos. The men refused but offered to sell the shot-gun. After some haggling over the price, an agreement was reached, and Ernest Dreger took the gun to the camp with him.

This trip to Northam had not been Dreger's only departure from the camp. On at least two other occasions he had borrowed a horse from Prowse and ridden to the town of Kellerberrin in search of Fred Johnson. The six men had clubbed together and taken a contract to clear Prowse's land. Johnson seemed to find the heavy physical work too demanding and uncongenial, and he slipped away whenever he could. Maren later accused him of laziness and failure to pull his weight. On another occasion Ernest Dreger had gone into Kellerberrin to prosecute another immigrant for non-payment of a debt. These three trips away from camp were destined to loom large in the immediate future of Ernest Dreger.

As a result of all the fighting and dissension caused by Sarah's presence, a major quarrel broke out in which Ernest Dreger attempted to intimidate both August Maren and Fred Johnson. The two men claimed that he had threatened to shoot them with his gun, although Adolf Dreger loyally asserted that his brother had only meant to punish them with his hands. Sarah Ligum's testimony on this point was studiously vague.[28] In the event, Fred Johnson was so frightened by what Ernest Dreger might do to him, that on the afternoon of 19 April he left the camp and travelled the 5 miles to his employer's house to inform him that he feared Ernest Dreger meant to kill him. The farmer telephoned the small Kellerberrin police station and informed Constable William McKay of what had taken place. Prowse volunteered to take Fred Johnson into his home for the night, although he expected trouble the next morning when he believed Dreger would come looking for Johnson. In order to forestall such an eventuality, McKay set out for Prowse's farm at 1.30 am next morning, reaching it just before daybreak. There he waited for Dreger's arrival. No one came. Eventually McKay rode on to the camp and quickly summed up the situation.

In Dreger's camp I found that there are six men and a young woman, they are all Letts (natives of a Russian Province), there [sic] *names are as follows: August Maren, Peter Older, Fread* [sic] *Johnson, Ernest Dreger, William Dreger, Adolf Dreger, and Sarah Ligum. The quarrel between Johnson and Ernest Dreger was over the girl who is living with Dreger as his wife and is jealous of Johnson* [sic]. *The other inmates of the camp told me that Dreger wished to fight with his hands and there was no mention of firearms or knives.*[29]

Before leaving Kellerberrin, McKay had been informed that a resident of the town had reported a stolen shot-gun, and his colleague Constable Cahill thought that it could well turn up at the Russians' camp. McKay soon found the shot-gun Dreger had purchased on his recent trip to Northam; it was the stolen gun. Dreger was arrested and charged with stealing and receiving. The main witness against him at his trial before two local justices of the peace was Fred Johnson, who swore that Ernest Dreger had travelled several times to Kellerberrin specifically to obtain the gun from a local butcher. Perhaps because he did not understand court procedure and did not bring forward any evidence on his own behalf from witnesses who had observed him with the gun in Northam, Dreger was found guilty and sentenced to three months' gaol with hard labour. But Dreger *had* been telling the truth, and the owner of the Northam Coffee Palace remembered Dreger obtaining the shot-gun after bargaining in his café with two other men.[30] Moreover, Adolf Dreger later testified that Fred Johnson had admitted lying in court in order to have Ernest sent to prison. Johnson claimed that August Maren had proposed perjury in an attempt to gain uninterrupted access to Sarah. Maren feared for his life if Ernest Dreger remained at liberty and discovered his renewed attentions to Sarah Ligum.

In the meantime, however, Ernest Dreger continued his prison sentence, an angry and embittered man. He had lost no time in informing Constable McKay that his erstwhile friends Maren and Johnson were Russian anarchists who had been involved in the celebrated Houndsditch murders, and McKay had dutifully included all this in his report of 21 April 1911. McKay also sent a note back to the camp with Fred Johnson, in which he notified Sarah Ligum that her protector had been gaoled for three months and instructed her to keep Adolf and William Dreger away from Maren and Johnson. Detective-Sergeant Joseph Frazer later reported that Sarah Ligum had moved into Maren's tent where she lived with him for a time before the police removed her to the care of the Salvation Army.[31] August Maren had achieved his immediate purpose in gratifying his desire for Sarah, but the cost of his sexual gratification was the disclosure of his connection with the Leesma organization and his subsequent imprisonment.

Ernest Dreger was convicted on 21 April 1911 and sent to Fremantle prison. The monthly Return of Prisoners for June 1911 shows that he was still there, although Detective-Sergeant Frazer's report indicates that shortly afterwards he was transferred to Rottnest Island Native Prison, 12 miles off the coast of Western Australia.

Ernest Dreger recognized that Maren and Johnson had trumped up the evidence that led to his conviction on a charge of stealing and receiving. While he served his sentence, his rancour against his former friends did not diminish. His conversations with fellow prisoners led them to believe that August Maren and Fred Johnson were notorious criminals from England. Not surprisingly, the prison authorities soon got wind of this. Dreger had already told Constable McKay about the Leesma connection with Maren and Johnson to no effect, and he was more than willing to repeat his allegations to the prison administrators. This time he received all the attention he could have desired, and a long and detailed statement was forwarded to the police.

The substance of Ernest Dreger's statement has been considered already. It filled in the details of August Maren's activities with the Leesma group and connected him directly with the murder of Leon Beron. From Sarah Ligum in the Salvation Army hostel in Perth the police obtained an account of recent events in London and Australia, and Adolf Dreger was interviewed also. These three statements, all separately obtained, reinforced one another and together they present a coherent and compelling account of Maren's involvement and illustrate that the boastful account of his activities did not vary much, whomever he spoke to.

The Western Australian police faced a dilemma regarding the information Dreger had given them. They decided to arrest Maren and Johnson and to hold them in custody long enough to allow urgent inquiries to be made by the London police into the allegations concerning the men. August Maren, traced to the town of Merredin, was arrested on 12 August 1911 and charged with conspiracy to present false evidence at the trial of Ernest Dreger. Fred Johnson had been found in Doodlakine and arrested on the same charge. The charge was sufficient to hold the two men whilst cables were sent to London and inquiries instituted there into the possibility that August Maren might actually have been Peter the Painter himself.

In Western Australia, as in London, it was the personality of Peter the Painter that overshadowed the entire proceedings. The public in Australia were every bit as susceptible to that 'apt and artful alliteration' to which Sir Melville Macnaghten, the head of CID Scotland Yard, had ascribed Peter's notoriety in England.[32] Somehow the news of August Maren's arrest and the substance of Ernest Dreger's allegations concerning him was leaked from the Western Australian police department to the local press, which was delighted that Western Australia should be the venue for such an exciting *cause célèbre*. The stories of the Houndsditch murders and the Sidney Street siege were retold and intense interest was aroused. The Perth weekend paper the *Sunday Times* published the results of some investigative journalism of its own, which involved interviewing an immigrant greengrocer who regularly received Polish newspapers from Warsaw. The greengrocer claimed that one of these papers had recently announced the arrest of Peter the Painter in Poland. This cast some doubts on Maren's identity as Peter the Painter, for as the journalist shrewdly pointed out, Peter could not be simultaneously under arrest in Warsaw and in Perth. It should be noted that it was the local press, not the Dregers or Sarah Ligum, which claimed that Maren was Peter Piaktow. The same paper carried a reported statement of Ernest Dreger's to the effect that there were at least twenty Russian anarchists in the country whom he knew personally and whose names he intended to give to the police. This allegation of such a large number of dangerous immigrants living in Australia filled the *Sunday Times* with foreboding and it was quick to draw the moral:

No doubt it will cause the authorities to be a little more careful over the nationality of our immigrants. Western Australia is up to date in most things, but we do not yet consider ourselves sufficiently advanced in civilization to have room for bombs and dynamitards. We will be always pleased to leave those to countries where the climate is colder but where the blood and the beer are both thicker. We have no time for them in sunny Australia, and woe betide the first man who introduces them. [33]

August Maren and Fred Johnson were transported to Perth and brought before a packed police court on the morning of 14 August, where they were remanded for eight days. The magistrate explained to both men that this involved their remaining in custody for another eight days before the police presented evidence against them on the charge of conspiracy. The morning newspaper commented on the fact that Maren and Johnson had been brought to Perth for trial on a charge which normally would have been heard in the local - in this case Kellerberrin - police court, and considered this to be an indication of the seriousness with which the authorities viewed Ernest Dreger's allegations. [34]

Control over the investigation into Dreger's charges and communication with the City of London police were vested in Chief-Inspector Connell of the Perth CID. Representatives of the press asked Connell whether he would comment publicly on the alleged identification of August Maren as Peter the Painter, and he replied with considerable asperity that he refused to pass any judgement based on newspaper speculation and had no intention of risking his reputation by adding to rumours of that sort: 'I am not going to be called a blithering idiot in a couple of months' time.' [35]

The impact of Peter the Painter on the general public was reflected in the correspondence received by the Western Australian police. They received one letter, written in Russian but signed in English, which followed the style of similar correspondence received by the police in London, with the possible exception that this letter came from a literate correspondent.

Mr Commissioner, Ha! Ha! Ha!

Yesterday I had the most heartfelt laugh at your expense because when you arrested Janson [Maren] and his comrade you thought that one of them was me. You made a great mistake. I will tell you openly and amicably that if they could not arrest me in the City of London where they have a very smart secret police I am certain you could never catch me in Australia today I'm here, tomorrow there and everywhere. I have sufficient money to take care of myself I arrived lately from South America if you think you can catch me you may try but just remember that I am no fool.

Your good friend
PETER the PAINTER. [36]

The parallels with London did not end there. In many ways Ernest and Adolf Dreger found themselves in a position somewhat akin to that of Nicolai Tomacoff's. While they waited for word from London on Maren's real identity and connection with the Lettish terrorists, the Western Australian police presented the Dregers with some gifts. Like Tomacoff, the Dregers found that the rewards for betraying their countrymen to the police were meagre. On 10 June 1911 Ernest Dreger received two shirts, a pair of trousers, two pairs of socks, two singlets, two pairs of underpants and another two pairs of socks. On 15 July he was given a pair of boots, more socks and underpants, two more shirts, dungaree trousers and a cap. This clothing was purchased by the Western Australian police for a total cost of £3.6.11. They also paid £1.1.0 to the Grand Central Coffee Palace in Perth for Dreger's accommodation from 14-17 July. Furthermore, both Ernest and Adolf Dreger received small cash payments during July and August 'for services re. undesirable immigrants'. These amounted to £3.5.0 for Ernest Dreger, and £1.16.0 for his brother Adolf.[37]

While the Dregers earned their emoluments and Sarah Ligum languished under the vigilant eye of the Salvation Army, the City of London police began following up the leads provided in the statements cabled to them from Western Australia. They traced Mrs Esther Ligum and Mr Louis Hersberg, and also several of Maren's acquaintances from whom they took statements, but these men all denied that they were connected in any way with anarchist outrages in London, or that they were anything more than honest, hard-working men. Maren was identified as a member of the Leesma organization, but the other allegations made by the Dregers and Sarah Ligum could not be substantiated adequately.

Unfortunately, August Maren had received some warning that the police were becoming interested in him. Adolf Dreger's statement disclosed that some time before his arrest, Maren had returned from a trip to Kellerberrin in a state of high excitement, brought about by a local policeman asking him questions about anarchists. This was most probably Constable McKay to whom Dreger had originally confided back in April. The questioning so alarmed Maren that he returned to the camp, built a large fire, and proceeded to burn all his correspondence and personal papers. The result was that when the Western Australian police did pounce on him, they found very little evidence other than a few photographs, and they did not recognize the importance of these. They did, however, intercept and confiscate all Maren's mail while he was in custody, and these letters remain in the files to this day. They are written in Lettish and remain untranslated because the police could find no one in Perth who could read Lettish. Most of this mail was personal, telling Maren of the sickness and death of his mother and asking his advice on the settlement of her meagre estate. But there is one letter of a frankly political nature which might indeed have come from his close friend Peter and Painter, who had been identified by the tsarist authorities as the Lett Janis Jacklis. The letter refers to industrial agitation in Poland and indicates that Maren's links with the anti-tsarist movement had not been broken by his migration to Australia.

Dear Friend!

My first lines are to inform you that today I have arrived in Stettin. All went smoothly only I was plagued severely by sea-sickness. For two days I did not eat at all and could not even look at food. After the second day I began to drink only cold water. With regard to the task, I have fulfilled all obligations. When no strength was left I climbed down to shovel coal and only lying down for five minutes to rest, occupied myself with the usual old thing. On the third day we came to a city where I began to recover a little. The rest of the days were beautiful and full of lovely sunshine. Altogether I spent eight days on this journey. I shall not write more about this because there are more serious things to write about.

The strike by the German seamen ended and at first they were not wanted back at their jobs but now they will be again accepted and Julius and myself will have to clear out in three or four days together with the other foreigners. There is no time for dreaming and the plans must be put into action or it may end as previously with the three pounds or even worse. I am asking you now to oblige and do me a favour perhaps for the last time. Please get some address in this city and some sort of connections in order to achieve desired results. I am sad, Comrade! Be kind and hurry because I have no prospect of income and in addition am suffering from the pocket tuberculosis [empty pockets - Lettish idiom]. *The amount of money is about two pounds sterling.*

I wanted to travel for one and a half months but it is not possible.

For the time being I have nothing else to write and shall end these lines wishing you all the best.

Janis.[38]

The two other personal letters from Maren's home in Kuldiga make mention of his sister Babina who seems also to have been linked with anti-tsarist movements in the Baltic through her relationship with a young activist described as 'a child of the Forest'. This is apparently a reference to the anarchist 'Forest Brothers' who were young revolutionaries waging a type of partisan campaign against the tsarist authorities after the failure of the 1905 Revolution.

Moreover, these letters reinforce the statements made by Ernest Dreger and by Maren himself that he had been in trouble with one of the local Russian nobles for his anti-tsarist views and had spent a considerable time in gaol before leaving the country and fleeing abroad. Dreger had affirmed that August Maren had been a schoolteacher 'until he got into trouble for being an anarchist. He was charged at Riga by some count with being an anarchist and was kept in prison for two years. They were unable to prove the charge as the principal witnesses disappeared and Maren was released.'[39] Maren admitted to the Western Australian police, in a voluntary account of his movements prior to immigrating to Australia, that he had spent the years from 1906 to 1908 in Goldingen Prison. He was brought before the Riga military court in November 1908 where the charge against him lapsed, and by New Year's Day in 1909 he was in Stockholm. The Swedish police apparently made him feel unwelcome despite his letter of recommendation from the socialist Hjalmer Branting, and Maren travelled the following day to Denmark where he remained for six months.[40] One of the Kuldiga letters discusses his chances of a return to Russia.

You wrote that you would like to return to Russia that would not be at all bad but you can never come to Kuldiga because the Lords who had that grudge against you could again start to persecute you and try to open old partly healed wounds which could again bring great pain. Because you journeyed to foreign lands that does not make you a fugitive you were legally freed and to tell the truth no one has enquired about you only for example the sister of the warden of the gaol has hinted that you left in time and the gossips think that a misfortune threatened you.[41]

There seems little doubt that August Maren had been an experienced revolutionary heavily involved in anti-tsarist activities in the Baltic region until his arrest in 1906. He was obviously implicated in the abortive 1905 Revolution, and his connection with the Leesma terrorists in London seems a natural progression from his earlier career.

Thus, prison was not new to Maren in 1911, nor were courts of law, and the published reports of proceedings in the Perth police court show that the experienced revolutionary did not accept his fate without a protest. On 30 August, when the two prisoners on remand were brought once more before the police court, Maren attempted to refute some of the evidence given the previous day by the Dregers and Sarah Ligum concerning his anarchist associates in London. He was at some pains to explain to the magistrate that the public meeting he had addressed in London had been a meeting of the Social Democrats and was not a function held at the anarchist club in Jubilee Street. He wanted it clearly understood that he had delivered no speeches in the Jubilee Street Club. The magistrate in reply advised Maren not to bother about such explanations because he faced a charge of conspiracy, not of being an anarchist, to which Maren responded by asserting that it was in his best interests to bother as he had heard that people thought he was Peter the Painter.[42]

As the hearing progressed, the magistrate informed Maren and

Johnson - who had become a silent spectator by this time - that their case would not come before the supreme court until early October. Maren complained bitterly at this delay. He regarded himself as an honest man and thought that the long delay between arrest and trial smacked more of the way such affairs were conducted in tsarist Russia than of Australia. The police prosecutor advised that he would not oppose the granting of substantial bail, and he noted that the Russian consul had interviewed the men and was watching the case on their behalf.

Maren: *'The Consul is only the servant of his Government. I have no friends here.'*
Mr Roe: *'You can have bail in one surety of £50, to be approved by me.'*
Maren made another voluble outburst, and said he considered that a distinction was being made between him and other suspected persons. The magistrate assured him that every person on remand, no matter of what nationality or the nature of the alleged offence, was treated alike. Finally Maren exclaimed, 'Right, I am going to die in this cell.'[43]

When the case came up again a week later, and the magistrate advised the two men to reserve their defense for the trial before the supreme court in October, August Maren complained that he would have spent two months in prison before actually being brought for trial.[44]

Maren and Johnson did more than just complain about the treatment they received. Although it was a carefully guarded secret and not a hint appeared in the press, the two men had begun a hunger strike in protest against the policy of deliberate delay by the Western Australian authorities in resolving their case before the courts. The fasting actually preceded Maren's outburst that he would die in his cell. The keeper of the Perth lock-up reported on 31 August 1911 that neither Maren nor Johnson had taken food or water since breakfast on the morning of the twenty-ninth, and that both men had expressed their determination to starve themselves. The keeper volunteered the opinion that the men appeared to resent being locked up and remanded so often. A doctor was called to examine both men, and he found Johnson weakening but Maren still resolutely refusing to take food or drink. His report ended on an ominous note: 'If he persists in his present intention I recommend that he be removed to the gaol hospital for forced feeding.'[45]

August Maren was a tenacious but not a foolhardy man. When faced with the unpleasant prospect of forced feeding at Fremantle prison hospital, he consented to break his long fast, and the keeper of the lock-up was happy to report on 2 October 1911 that both prisoners were now taking their food and medicine, that they were also consuming extra food ordered by the doctor, and that he did not anticipate any further trouble with them before their trial in four days' time.[46]

August Maren and Fred Johnson had been arrested on 12 August

1911, and many weeks had elapsed while the Western Australian police
department waited for word from London. If Maren proved to be Peter
the Painter or to have been connected with the Houndsditch murders
and the siege of Sidney Street, then they would hold him in detention
until the City of London police made arrangements for his extradition.
The delays which Maren so resented were deliberate ploys, designed to
kill time until a firm response was received from London. Eventually, the
British police reluctantly acknowledged that they had no evidence to
justify Maren's extradition. Certainly, he had been identified as a close
friend of Peter Piaktow's, but the British authorities had also been forced
to concede that they could not extradite even Peter the Painter, let alone
his associates. The charges of conspiracy brought against the surviving
members of Leesma group 5 had all failed, and there seemed little chance
of similar charges against other members of the organization proving any
more successful. Grudgingly, they admitted that they possessed no
evidence to link August Maren or Fred Johnson with the Houndsditch
murders, the Clapham Common killing, or the Sidney Street siege, and
requested that no action be taken on behalf of the City of London
police.[47]

The immediate consequence of the English inquiries was that the
Western Australian police department was left in an invidious position. It
had acted prematurely in arresting August Maren and Fred Johnson on
what can only be described as a 'bogus' charge. When other foreign law
enforcement agencies imagined they had traced the elusive Peter the
Painter, they usually contacted London and asked whether arrest and
extradition should proceed. To each such request the London police
responded in the negative. In this case, however, the Western Australian
police force had acted precipitately and had contacted London only after
the suspects had been secured. The responsibility for the arrests lay in
Western Australia and the hollowness of the conspiracy charges can be
judged from the fact that the Crown did not proceed with them and, after
holding Maren and Johnson in custody for almost two months, entered a
nolle prosequi [stay of proceedings] and dropped the action. The two
men were released immediately and permitted to sink back into
obscurity.

These were the major but not the only involvement of Australia in the
activities of the Leesma organization and the incidents of December 1910
and January 1911 in London. In 1913 the City of London police heard
once more from Australia, this time from New South Wales. On 14
August 1913, Ernest Day, Inspector-General of Police, wrote to the commissioner of police for the City of London, enclosing the fingerprints and
nine photographs of a man named Max Selling, currently under arrest in
New South Wales on a charge of forging banknotes. One of the photographs seemed to Inspector-General Day to bear a striking resemblance
to the pictures of Peter the Painter, circulated by the British authorities
after the Houndsditch murders. Day requested confirmation of the iden-

tification and advice as to what action London desired. These photographs are no longer in the London files, but there is a note to the effect
that they had been shown to Mr and Mrs Katz, who had been the landlords at 59 Grove Street, and both had stated that Selling was not Peter
Piaktow. Moreover, the fingerprints allowed the London authorities to
make a positive identification, and Max Selling was found to be the
known criminal Johan Kaikon. This information was forwarded to New
South Wales with a request that no action be taken on behalf of the City
of London.[48]

Australia reappears in the Houndsditch files in 1917, when the commissioner of police for the City of Melbourne in Victoria cabled his coun-
terpart in London that his officers believed they had located Peter the
Painter in Melbourne and desired that all information in the possession
of the London police regarding this man be telegraphed immediately.
This cable carries a revealing note from a Detective-Sergeant Henry
Dupe that 'the files relating to the Houndsditch Murders have been
searched and no trace of any previous communication from Australia
can be found.'[49] It does not reflect much credit on the slap-dash book-
keeping methods or filing procedures of the London police. The cable in
reply was brief and to the point. It stated incorrectly that no further
particulars were known about Peter the Painter, and concluded: 'Do not
arrest for me.'

The Melbourne police refused to be fobbed off so easily. On 12
September 1917 a letter was despatched to London enclosing a photograph of their suspect, an immigrant chef named Paul Hubert. Hubert
sounds a fascinating and eccentric character in his own right. He had
been involved in the grisly double murder of two Russian dancers in
Sydney in 1913 and had moved to Melbourne with something of a cloud
still over his name. He was known to be an expert pistol shot and knife
thrower, and he had given public demonstrations of his prowess with
both weapons. The police believed him to be of Russian origin, although
Hubert himself claimed to be French. The photograph shows that
Hubert did bear a striking resemblance to Peter the Painter, although he
does look considerably older. The police in London, who showed
Hubert's photograph to all the people still available who had any
connection with the Houndsditch case, including Mrs Katz, were
unanimous that Hubert was not Peter Piaktow. These findings were
summarized in a letter sent to Melbourne on 12 December 1917, and
here Paul Hubert fades out of the story, together with the Melbourne
police authorities.

The 'blessed land of Australia' did gain one more piece of publicity as
the temporary abode of Peter the Painter in 1934, when the former
Detective-Sergeant Benjamin Leeson - the policeman who had first
arrested Sara Trassjonsky, and who had been shot in the back during the
brick-throwing episode at the siege of Sidney Street - published an
extravagantly self-serving autobiography. Leeson's recovery from his

wound had been slow, and he had been invalided out of the police force. His doctors ordered a sea voyage to repair his broken health, and later in 1911 Leeson took a voyage to Australia. Although he claimed that he wanted a quiet life, Leeson contrived to let so many of his fellow passengers know of his role in the Sidney Street siege, that they nick-named him 'Peter the Painter'. In his autobiography, Leeson claimed that a secret international red brotherhood of anarchists existed, whose long arm reached even to Australia. When his ship called at Albany in Western Australia, he was accosted by 'two foreign-looking individuals', who asked him whether anyone called Leeson had come ashore. The vigilant and alert ex-policeman immediately recognized that something odd was afoot, and cleverly informed his interlocutors that the man called Leeson had decided to remain on board.

With that they moved off, but the incident had made me a trifle thoughtful. After all I hadn't come thousands of miles in search of health merely to run into the arms of my Russian friends from the East End again. I was not 'on duty'. I was all for a quiet life. I regained my ship, and was not sorry when she sailed. But I had not thrown off my pursuers. [50]

Leeson asserts that these dubious foreigners followed his ship to Melbourne where he was once more accosted by them and asked whether a man called Leeson had disembarked. Once again, the native wit of the former London bobby proved more than a match for such foreign riff-raff, and he threw them off the scent with false information. He never saw them again.

Leeson's breathtaking adventure did not end in Melbourne, however, for the best was yet to come. On reaching Sydney, he decided to take an excursion by train into the Blue Mountains, close to the city. On the day of his departure, as he purchased his ticket at Central Station in Sydney, whom should he see but Peter the Painter himself? Leeson claimed that he recognized him immediately because he knew Peter very well by sight, having often seen him in the saloon-bar of the Kings Head Public House on the corner of Grove Street and Commercial Road in the East End. This claim is nothing more than arrant nonsense. The City of London police records show that until photographs of Peter Piaktow had been obtained from the French police, the British authorities possessed only the vaguest and most general of descriptions of this elusive will-o'-the-wisp. All the evidence on file shows that Peter was a quiet, reserved, shy person, who made little contact with anyone outside the Leesma group. He is never mentioned in any part of the documents as being known to frequent public houses, or of carousing in the company of city detectives. Leeson's flight of fancy did not stop there, for after he had purchased his ticket, he was joined in his compartment by Peter the Painter.

100
'THE
BLESSED
LAND OF
AUS-
TRALIA'

We were alone. I guessed that he would be armed, and sundry straying of his hand to his hip-pocket, as if to assure himself of the readiness of his gun to his hand, confirmed my guess. Neither of us gave any sign of recognition, merely passing the time of day and sundry other remarks of little importance. 'Do you come from England?' asked the Painter. 'Yes,' said I, and a silence fell. It was an awkward situation. There was I, alone with an armed desperado who knew who I was, and who knew that I knew who he was. He could not, of course, guess that I was not in Australia on any official mission or that my connection with the Force had been severed through my wound. Further, he could not know that, so far as he was concerned, there was no jot of evidence to prove his participation in either the Houndsditch or Sidney Street affairs, however gravely the finger of suspicion might point towards him.

To his way of thinking, I must have represented the long arm of the Law, stretched out to haul him back from that far continent.

It was a tense moment, he wondering when I was going to show my hand, I asking myself how soon I should be looking down the barrel of a revolver. But nothing happened.

My destination was a place named Wentworth Falls, and though I would have liked to extract a little information from Peter as to his movements after Sidney Street, I was not exactly sorry when the train lumbered into the station.

Perfunctory farewells on either side, and I stepped out on to the platform, leaving Peter to travel - who knows where?[51]

Leeson's stories can safely be regarded as inventions designed to pad out and make interesting a mediocre autobiography, written over twenty years after the events it purports to describe. The entire account is full of fabrications and factual inaccuracies, even to the point where he gives the wrong address for the rooms shared by Peter the Painter, Fritz Svaars and Luba Milstein. Not one of these Australian adventures occurred within sight of witnesses, and Leeson made no report of them to the local or the English police. It is possible that he travelled through Western Australia at the time when August Maren's case was receiving such widespread local publicity, and when Australian journalists indulged themselves by speculating on the identification of Maren as Peter Piaktow. Leeson's story could easily have been concocted twenty-three years later from vague memories of this episode. Leeson's reminiscences do indicate, however, the continuing domination of Peter the Painter when the events of late 1910 and early 1911 were discussed, and provide a measure of the degree to which fascination with this one personality has lingered and added to the reputation for daring and resourcefulness; whilst the names of those who were physically involved in the Tottenham, Houndsditch, Sidney Street and Clapham Common affairs, have long since been forgotten.

FOOTNOTES

101
'THE
BLESSED
LAND OF
AUS-
TRALIA'

1 *The Times*, 20 December 1910.
2 Conversations with Mr Valdemar Vilder and Mr Aldis Putnins during 1978-79.
3 A.T. Yarwood, *Asian Migration to Australia: The Background to Exclusion 1896-1923*, Melbourne, 1968, pp. 42-3.
4 Prime Minister's Department CRS. A2 Correspondence Files, file 14/466/4 Immigration, 1908.
5 Prime Minister's Department CRS. A2 Correspondence Files, file 14/466/2 Immigration, 1912-15.
6 South Australia and Tasmania did not offer assisted passages at this time, although South Australia revived its assisted passage scheme early in 1911. For details of the revived system see *The Times*, 21 February 1911.
7 Prime Minister's Department CRS. A2 Correspondence Files, file 14/466/4 Immigration, 1908.
8 Houndsditch Papers.
9 Houndsditch Papers and Western Australian Police Department Papers, file 3911/1911.
10 Western Australian Police Department Papers, file 3911/1911.
11 ibid.
12 ibid.
13 Houndsditch Papers.
14 *Daily Chronicle*, 22 December 1910.
15 Houndsditch Papers.
16 Michael Futrell, op. cit., pp. 35-41.
17 Western Australian Police Department Papers, file 3911/1911.
18 Houndsditch Papers.
19 Western Australian Police Department Papers, file 3911/1911.
20 See for example Eric Linklater, *The Corpse on Clapham Common: A Tale of Sixty Years Ago*, London, 1971.
21 See the note written in prison by Karl Hoffman to Yourka Dubof, Houndsditch Papers.
22 Donald Rumbelow, op. cit., pp. 179-80.
23 Houndsditch Papers.
24 ibid.
25 Passenger lists for immigrant ships are kept in the J.S. Battye Library, State Library, Western Australia.
26 Western Australian Police Department Papers, file 3911/1911.
27 ibid.
28 ibid.
29 ibid.
30 ibid.
31 ibid.
32 See above.
33 *Sunday Times*, 20 August 1911.
34 *West Australian*, 19 August 1911.
35 *Daily News*, 14 August 1911.

102
'THE
BLESSED
LAND OF
AUS-
TRALIA'

36   Western Australian Police Department Papers, file 3911/1911.
37   ibid.
38   ibid.
39   ibid.
40   ibid.
41   ibid.
42   *West Australian*, 31 August 1911.
43   ibid.
44   *West Australian*, 8 September 1911.
45   Western Australian Police Department Papers, file 3911/1911.
46   ibid.
47   Houndsditch Papers. *See also* Agent General for Western Australia, file 1230.
48   Houndsditch Papers.
49   ibid.
50   Benjamin Leeson, *Lost London*, London, 1934, p. 219.
51   ibid., pp. 219-22.

5
AFTERMATH – THE ROAD TO RESTRICTION

The Tottenham outrage, the Houndsditch murders, the Clapham Common murder, and the siege of Sidney Street had an immense impact on public opinion both in Britain and abroad, and a wide cross-section of the British populace found themselves emotionally caught up in the investigations and the public mourning for the three dead policemen. Thousands of Londoners lined the streets leading to St Paul's Cathedral to pay their last respects to the three men who received the hitherto unprecedented honour of a public funeral attended by the king's personal representative, by the Home Secretary Winston Churchill, and by all the high dignitaries of Church and State then resident in London. The funeral became a social occasion, and the commissioner of police found himself seriously embarrassed at having to refuse a great many applications for seats in the cathedral.[1]

Such a public display of grief was noteworthy enough in its own right, but a more deep-rooted impression had been made both on individuals and on the public at large that should now be examined. To begin with, there was a renewal of calls for restriction of immigration from Europe which echoed the earlier agitation of the British Brothers' League. To some commentators the affairs of Tottenham, Houndsditch and Sidney Street provided ample evidence to substantiate the claim that the Aliens Restriction Act of 1905 - as it was administered by the Liberal government - was insufficient to protect the British public from periodic bouts of politically inspired lawlessness. It has been noted already that the popular press indulged in a xenophobic campaign against foreigners from Eastern Europe once the involvement of immigrants in the Houndsditch murders was suspected. As early as 21 December 1910, *The Times* published a letter to the editor, which called for compulsory registration of aliens by the local police. This letter was followed by others in support of the general principle that foreigners were not in Britain by right, but by the grace of the British people; that they possessed no inaliable rights other than those the British people chose to give them; and that, since Englishmen who travelled on the continent were often obliged to register with the local authorities when they first moved into an area there

104
AFTER-
MATH -
THE ROAD
TO
RESTRIC-
TION
could be no legitimate objections if Britain chose to exercise similar rights over aliens within her hospitable shores. Nor should such immigrants be permitted to continue using Britain as a secure base for the organization of anti-tsarist campaigns in their homelands, for the recent outrages showed too clearly the result of such indulgence. One of the paper's own correspondents illustrated how such a political group could begin by being interested in combatting continental autocracy, yet end by discharging firearms in London.

When the Russian Anarchist leaders settled in London they began to carry on their propaganda here. For some time they have circulated violent revolutionary literature among their fellow-countrymen in the East End. Only a few days before the Houndsditch crime I chanced to visit Spitalfields, and glancing in a small bookshop there, saw and purchased a series of Russian postcards, printed in Whitechapel. One showed the Tsar standing trembling before the headless Louis. Another depicted him as the instigator of the flogging of women, the shooting of old men, and the crushing of liberty. Others were to the same effect. In the Anarchist meetings that have been freely held, the policy of 'direct action' has been openly advocated . . . Meetings are frequently held at the Anarchist Clubs. Various anniversaries -notably the establishment of the French Commune and the death of the Chicago 'martyrs' - are strictly observed. The visitors are mostly foreigners. Some time since, I attended a special gathering in a little hall off Brick Lane, Whitechapel. A Spaniard declaimed with great vigour in his own tongue against the Government of King Alfonso; a French woman led the 'Marseillaise' in French; then a swarthy and handsome man, evidently a Spaniard, mounted the platform, revolver in hand. The chairman explained that his comrade could not talk, but would show us the best way to use a revolver. The man thereupon shot over our heads at a target at the other end of the hall and gave a really pretty exhibition of small-arm firing. The gathering terminated with a dance. [2]

The core of the trouble, it was alleged, lay with the government's failure to enforce the inept restrictive legislation already on the statute books, and a campaign was launched to highlight the glaring inadequacies of the existing statutes. The Aliens Restriction Act empowered the home secretary to exempt immigrants from inspection, and the practice had arisen where the only aliens scrutinized by the authorities were those who arrived from European and Mediterranean ports. Thus, a man like Fritz Svaars, who escaped from America to London with a price on his head, would have slipped through the net without undergoing inspection. Again, the Act and its regulations specifically exempted a large range of incoming passengers from official observation. Among these were passengers in 'non-immigrant ships', that is ships which carried twenty

aliens or less as steerage passengers; passengers from 'extra-European' ports; all cabin passengers; second-class passengers except those from Hamburg, Bremen, Rotterdam and a few other ports; transmigrants passing through the country en route to other destinations; immigrants who intended to proceed 'within a reasonable time' to some destination outside the United Kingdom; passengers who held return-tickets to foreign countries; seamen; alien residents who were returning to their homes in Britain; and immigrants who were fleeing from religious or political persecution. 105
AFTER-
MATH -
THE ROAD
TO
RESTRIC-
TION Immigrants who were not included in any of these categories were inspected and were liable to be denied entry to the country on any of the following grounds: if they could not show that they possessed or could obtain adequate means of support; if they were lunatics, idiots or subject to disease or infirmity; if they had committed crimes for which they could be extradited; or if expulsion orders had already been served upon them under the Act.

It is obvious that the Leesma Letts, together with their Russian and Jewish accomplices, and indeed nearly every refugee from the Russian empire, could qualify for unrestricted entry into Britain because they were victims of religious and political persecution. Nor was this situation a new one. As early as 1894, following the anarchist assassination of President Carnot of France, the former British Prime Minister, Lord Salisbury, asserted in the House of Lords that the killing had been planned in Britain, which had earned the censure of all the European powers because it permitted such enterprises to be 'prepared and organized on this soil'.

We know there are large clubs of persons in this country, or there have been, in which these murderous plots have been hatched and brought to completion; so that now England is to a great extent the headquarters, the base, from which the Anarchist operations are conducted, the laboratory in which all their contrivances are perfected.[3]

The Leesma organization fitted this description with the one important difference being that hitherto the alien political groups had refrained from abusing British hospitality. The Leesma Letts had broken the unwritten law that expropriations or any other form of activity which might jeopardize the continued existence of the British haven should be eschewed. By murdering English policemen and engaging in shooting matches in the streets of London, the Leesma people endangered not only themselves and their continued existence as a fighting group, but all other refugees who feared forcible repatriation to Russia more than any other fate. It comes as no surprise then to find that the other refugee organizations and indeed the Lettish Social Democrats were quick to dissociate themselves publicly from such a tainted and potentially dangerous group. If Ochrana secret agents were involved they could not have acted more cunningly than to trick credulous men into striking at the heart of

106
AFTER-
MATH -
THE ROAD
TO
RESTRIC-
TION

the very society that gave them protection. Houndsditch and Sidney Street placed at risk the future of Britain as a refuge for anti-tsarist revolutionaries. The organizers of the Jubilee Street Club were the first to recognize this danger and attempted to distance themselves from the Letts involved with an announcement in *The Times* on 7 January 1911.

The different groups that are united in the International Federation do not approve of acts such as those of the Houndsditch murders . . . so far as we can judge, either from the names published or the photograph printed, they were certainly not members of our club in Jubilee Street. The police tell us that they attended our meetings. That may be so, and it is possible that they belonged to one of the Lettish groups which work independently, apparently preferring to keep themselves aloof from other anarchists here. The Houndsditch act bears a strong resemblance to a number of 'expropriations' which took place in Russia during the revolutionary movement, and which were afterwards condemned and discouraged by the Anarchists themselves. The murderers were young fellows who were caught up in the expropriation movement in Russia. It would not be at all surprising if these men had been to our club meetings or lectures, had come in contact with a Russian police agent provocateur *there, and had been urged on by him to do what they did, in order to help to rob us of our homes in the last country open to the political refugee. Similar work has been done by Russian police agents in Belgium, in Paris, and elsewhere during the past few years, as we know. But Anarchists as a whole are now against private expropriation, for we realize the harm it has done us.*[4]

The following week it was the turn of the Lettish Social Democrats to abandon the men publicly, though the party did provide defense counsel for Jacob Peters and Osip Federoff when the two men ultimately came to trial. The statement released by the party also drew attention to the possible existence of an *agent provocateur*.

In connexion with the horrible deeds committed in Houndsditch and Sidney Street, Stepney, statements have appeared in the English Press which tend to put the blame for these atrocities on the Lettish Social Democratic Party. We feel bound to protest against such aspersions in the most energetic manner, and to declare that we have nothing in common with robbers and hooligans who so frequently are influenced by Russian police agents; nor can we be held responsible for their deeds. We wish to point out that at the Congress of the Russian Social-Democratic Party, held in London in May, 1907, in which delegates of our organization took part, a special resolution was passed by which members of the party were expressly forbidden to have anything whatever to do with 'expropriators' (robbers of public or private property). This resolution has been strictly carried out in our organization, and in

doing so we have acted vigorously against any one palliating or
excusing such means of carrying on our struggle.

We express the conviction that the English democracy will distinguish between criminal hooligans and convinced Socialists, and that it will not put the responsibility for the criminal misdeeds of individuals upon a Social-Democratic Party. We are also firmly convinced that the English democracy will not abandon its glorious tradition of affording protection to political refugees, and will not withdraw its sympathy and support from our struggle against Russian despotism.[5]

Both these statements allude to the existence of a prejudice against tsarism in the British people, a prejudice that is well illustrated in the contemporary newspapers. Tsarist autocracy was held widely to be the most savagely repressive form of society existing at that time, and the liberal English press did not disguise its sympathy for the anti-tsarist cause. Indeed, hatred of tsarism had become so widespread a phenomenon amongst the English-speaking democracies that the Russian authorities had given up attempting to secure the extradition of captured criminals for trial in Russia. Such attempts only provoked an intense and popular agitation against Russia while failing to achieve the desired deportation. It was better not to request extradition that to risk alienating public opinion in the democracies.[6] England's harbouring of escaped murderers and expropriators, however, obviously offended many educated Russians, one of whom wrote to express her disgust with what she clearly regarded as yet another blatant example of British double standards.

A Yiddish-speaking man may be a Russian subject, but he is no more a real Russian on that account than a Hottentot, being a British subject, is a real Englishman. In the second place, permit me to remark that, although we Russians may be as bad as some of your papers describe us, we have at least one virtue which you do not seem to recognize: we do our utmost to prevent murderers, thieves and burglars, and other criminals crossing our frontier. No Russian subject is allowed to leave Russia without a passport, which is never granted to any known criminal. If any such criminals evade our vigilance, our police are only too anxious to inform your police and solicit their co-operation in the arrest of the fugitive. But such offenders have only to allege that they are political refugees to be welcomed by your people and protected by your authorities. In your eyes, murder is no murder when the victim is a Russian policeman. But when the same criminals kill an English policeman you do not seem to see it in quite the same light.

Try to put yourself in our place. What would you think if 'Peter the Painter' were welcomed at St Petersburg, and if our Government refused to give him up, because he had only killed an English police-

108
AFTER-
MATH -
THE ROAD
TO
RESTRIC-
TION

man and was therefore entitled to a right of asylum as a political refugee? Of course such a crime against civilization is unthinkable on the part of the Russian Government, but it would represent only too faithfully the position which England has always been proud to maintain before the world.

What I want to know is whether, now that you are suffering a very, very small part of the misery which these murderers have inflicted on us, you are willing to co-operate with the police of the world in extirpating this murderous gang of ruthless murderers? If you are, you will find ready co-operation on our side; if you are not, then, I fear, the world will say that you care nothing for murder so long as it is only Russian police, generals, or ministers who are murdered, and you will remain in the future, as in the past, the refuge and the shelter of the assassins of the world![7]

Repressive legislation was not immediately forthcoming, and the British government retained a shaky equilibrium. This failure to bring down reactionary legislation, however, does not preclude the existence of *agents provocateurs* within the Leesma organization, who plotted a series of crimes specifically designed to provoke such legislation and thereby deny British sanctuary to terrorists on the run. Nor does the lack of repressive enactments mean that they were not seriously considered. The coroner's report into the death of Sergeant Bentley contained recommendations that were not acted upon by the British government, but which went far in the direction of repression and gave a sure indication of public opinion on this vexed question. The Coroner, Dr Waldo, admitted that there seemed little that could be done to frame any effective measure for the exclusion of criminals short of preventing the entry of all foreigners. In the admission of a given number of aliens there were bound to be some criminals. The question facing the British authorities was whether the size of the criminal element warranted special legislative controls. The Houndsditch affair made it tragically self-evident that the current system had not succeeded. In any case, expulsion was wisdom after the event and a remedy only when the criminal was captured and convicted. An Aliens Restriction Act would not be necessary at all if some system for international police control of criminal aliens founded on the scientific method of fingerprint identification were operative.

Until international co-operation of that sort eventuated, the British faced the problem of regulating and controlling the increasing number of immigrants. According to Dr Waldo, the first logical step in obtaining control over resident aliens in Britain was to establish a method of registration and supervision for a fixed number of years after their arrival in the country. The registration procedures ought to include fingerprint identification and systematic, compulsory personal report at intervals over six years. Failure to comply was to be a punishable offence, and if repeated would constitute grounds for deportation. Dr Waldo also suggested that the law be altered to ensure that possession of deadly weapons by any alien was forbidden under all circumstances, and that any breach of this regulation was to be punishable by fine and imprisonment for a first offence, and by permanent deportation for a second offence.[8]

109
AFTER-
MATH -
THE ROAD
TO
RESTRIC-
TION

In the event, Dr Waldo's recommendations and the public campaign in favour of restrictive legislation against aliens was ignored by the government, which treated the matter as a storm in a teacup. The implementation of such suggestions was considered to be too expensive, although ironically something very like them was to be introduced in 1914 when Britain entered the war. But the city coroner received substantial public support from Sir Robert Anderson, one of the most eminent police officials in England.[9]

For a time it appeared as though the strength of public opinion would over-ride party differences and succeed in forcing legislation through the British parliament, despite the reluctance of Asquith's Liberal government of the day. On 3 February 1911 a conservative backbencher E.A. Goulding brought matters to a head when he introduced a bill that provided for the compulsory registration of all immigrants subject to inspection under the Act of 1905; empowered the Home Secretary to expel any alien convicted of a criminal offence; forbade refugees to possess firearms without a licence; and reduced to one the number of immigrants necessary to define a vessel as an immigrant ship. In order to circumvent this proposed repressive legislation, Winston Churchill was forced to bring forward a limited measure sponsored by the government, which was designed primarily to prevent crime by refugees and to facilitate their expulsion if convicted. Compulsory registration did not form part of Churchill's bill, nor was the right to political asylum infringed. Both the government bill and Goulding's private member's bill bogged down in the committee stages, and the developing crisis in Europe increasingly occupied public and parliamentary attention.

By August 1914 the war was the chief concern of the House of Commons and an even greater alien threat to Britain than the Leesma organization cast a shadow over the country. On 5 August 1914, as a matter of national urgency, an Aliens Restriction Bill was introduced. This bill, which remains the basis of British immigration policy to this day, required all aliens to register with the police, and gave the Home Secretary power to deport or exclude any alien without appeal. Unlike the earlier bills, this new enactment was passed in a day, and although the government during the debate gave a firm and unequivocal undertaking that the Act would remain in force only for the duration of the national emergency, its life has been extended indefinitely and it continues to govern the admission of immigrants to England. All aliens resident in England must be registered, and the Home Secretary or the courts can order any alien deported whenever it is deemed conducive to the public good.

110
AFTER-
MATH -
THE ROAD
TO
RESTRIC-
TION

British involvement in the European Economic Community, however, will inevitably lead to changes in immigration restriction. But the principle that the nation had a right to control immigration - established originally in 1905 and massively reinforced by the Leesma operations between 1909 and 1911 prior to the thorough-going legislation of 1914 - will probably always form the basis of future enactments. The activities of the Leesma organization and the subsequent mobilization of British public opinion against immigrants led the way to permanent restrictive legislation, which by 1914 had become as repressive as the Ochrana could have desired. Within three years of the final Leesma stand at Sidney Street, anti-alien restriction and control was firmly enshrined on the statute books, and with public support it was enacted without protest and has remained substantially unchallenged ever since.

Nor was the Leesma impact on restrictive immigration confined to Britain. The Commonwealth of Australia's immigration polices were affected also. When the Australian colonies united in federation in 1901, the new federal government had been empowered to make laws for the entire nation with respect to immigration and emigration. The earlier legislation which had been enacted by the colonial legislatures in these areas remained in operation or at least on the statute books. Moreover, because the various states in the new federation already possessed the bureaucratic apparatus to administer their immigration laws, it was felt to be an unnecessary duplication for the commonwealth to recruit a separate staff of its own. Accordingly, the former state officials transferred to the federal public service and administered the common-wealth's immigration legislation in addition to that previously enacted by the state governments.[10] The individual states, with the exception of Tasmania and South Australia, ran their own immigration services in London, and took responsibility for the calibre of immigrants travelling to Australia on assisted or nominated passages. In February 1911 the government of South Australia fell into line with the other states and revived the provisions of its old pre-federation Immigration Act with its standard offer of attractive assisted passages for immigrants who matched the state's requirements.[11] The following month Queensland followed suit and offered an assistance scheme that was significantly cheaper than those available from the representatives of the other Australian states.[12] All this activity by the Australian states shows clearly that they were competing with one another for immigrants, and their subsidies tended to rise and fall in relation to what was on offer from their rivals. Similarly, the Australian states were in competition with Canada and South Africa for British immigrants, and the financial contribution demanded of the nominators of immigrants tended to be fairly low in reflection of international competition in addition to the internecine interstate rivalry previously noted. Ernest Dreger took advantage of this situation when he travelled to Perth to nominate August Maren and Sarah Ligum in 1910. He was pleasantly surprised to find that the price had fallen so low, and he immediately added his two brothers to his list of applicants for nominated passages.[13]

111
AFTER-
MATH -
THE ROAD
TO
RESTRIC-
TION

Strictly speaking, Ernest Dreger ought not to have been permitted to nominate anybody. The Western Australian regulations specified that nominees had to be residents of the United Kingdom or of a British self-governing colony to qualify for the scheme, and the obvious intention of the legislators had been to restrict the scheme to people of British nationality. The flood of immigrants from central and eastern Europe into London's East End, however, had produced an entire group of non-British people who were nonetheless British residents. They might not have been the first choice in the rush for immigrants, but in a competitive situation the Australian states could not afford to scrutinize too closely the antecedents of immigrants who satisfied the conditions and applied for assisted passage from Britain.

Refugees from Russia's Baltic provinces did possess one qualification which obviously outweighed the shortcoming of their ethnicity. At least they were white and could therefore rely on a comparatively warm welcome when they reached their new home in Australia. Before federation, racially based immigration restrictions had been operative in all the Australian colonies, but had been directed specifically at Asian migration. Indeed, some writers have seen Australian fears of an overwhelming Asian immigration as a powerful stimulus to federation. But such restrictions were never intended to apply to European immigration, which was encouraged by all the Australian colonial governments.[14] At federation there had been consensus amongst the Australian colonies that coloured races were to be kept out of the new nation, and that complexion rather than culture was to form the basis for administrative judgements in this area. In the commonwealth government files on immigration there is a booklet of confidential instructions for staff charged with the responsibility of administering immigration procedures in the years prior to the First World War. These directions make it perfectly clear that Baltic Europeans satisfied the main criteria for entry into Australia.

The object of this Act (Immigration Restriction Act) is to prevent the admission to the Commonwealth of undesirable immigrants. For practical purposes these may be divided into three classes, viz.:
(a) persons of coloured races;
(b) persons likely to become a charge on the state; and
(c) persons suffering from diseases of certain classes.
On the arrival at the first port of call in the Commonwealth of vessels from abroad, an examination of all passengers on board should be made by the officers. All coloured persons who are not exempted by the Act, or who are not in possession of other papers entitling them to admission must be closely examined, and unless the case presents some special features which would justify reference to the Collector, they

112

AFTER-
MATH -
THE ROAD
TO
RESTRIC-
TION

must be asked to pass the dictation test . . . Solicitors or other agents must not be permitted to be present at examinations by Customs officers for the purpose of inquiring into the right of coloured persons to admission to the Commonwealth.

It is intended that the dictation test, which is to meet the case of coloured persons desiring to enter the Commonwealth, shall be an absolute bar to admission. Officers will therefore take means to ascertain whether, in their opinion, the immigrant can write English. If it is thought that he can, the test must be dictated in some other European language, one with which the immigrant is not acquainted.[15]

The significance of the case of August Maren, a self-confessed member of the Leesma terrorists, can be better appreciated when it is realized that his involvement with such a notorious group was to be the case of a break in the previous accord between commonwealth and states over immigration and was to lead Western Australia into fundamental revisions in restrictionist thinking. The possibility that Maren might have been Peter the Painter, the publicity given to Ernest Dreger's statement that he personally knew of more than twenty anti-tsarist terrorists living incognito in Australia, and the first substantial period in office of the state branch of the Australian Labor Party, fortuitously coincided. The new government was not acquainted with political realities, having assumed office only a few months before the anarchist scare broke, and the cabinet was inexperienced. The anti-alien publicity in Western Australia was as virulent as much that appeared in the London press at the time of the Houndsditch, Sidney Street and Clapham Common affairs, and the state government's panic was reflected in important alterations to the regulations governing the assisted and nominated systems of immigration which stressed that cultural background was equally as important in the selection of immigrants as colour. On 21 August 1911, the colonial secretary in Perth instructed the Western Australian agent general in London that the Ernest Dreger case was not to be repeated.

In order that there may be no possibility of such cases arising in the future, it has been decided that no Russians or Russian Jews, whether resident in England or elsewhere, are to be approved as Nominated Immigrants, nor are any other foreigners to be accepted about whose desirability there is any doubt.

In regard to foreigners other than Russians, enquiry will in future be made into the character and circumstances of the Nominators, and I shall be greatly obliged if you will also have special enquiry made as regards the Nominees before granting passages.[16]

Nor were these major alterations in procedure a temporary phenomenon. Rather, they found their way into the advertisement handbills distributed to prospective immigrants to Western Australia when they sought

information from the agent general's office in London, and became one of the most important reasons for the disqualification of would-be immigrants seeking nominated passages to Western Australia. The handbills listed those classes of people ineligible for such assistance: 113
AFTER-
MATH -
THE ROAD
TO
RESTRIC-
TION

Persons who have previously resided in Western Australia.

Persons who are physically or mentally unsound, or who are in any way deformed, or who are not of good moral repute, or who have been in any habitual receipt of parish relief, or who are of Asiatic or African African origin.

Males, married women, and widows over 45 years of age.

Single women over 35 years of age.

No person who is not a naturalized British subject will be eligible to apply for nominated passages for any person. [17]

What emerges from this episode is that the Western Australian state govenment was panicked into altering its immigration policy to one that not only discriminated on the basis of colour, but also on the basis of culture. Colour remained a permanent barrier, but culture became a temporary one. It was envisaged that non-British Europeans could become worthy members of the Anglo-Saxon or Anglo-Celtic civilization, provided they were given sufficient time to raise themselves to that elevated cultural plateau. Hence the ban was not complete. Baltic Europeans who proved their worthiness by attaining naturalization were permitted to nominate their friends or families, but non-British subjects were excluded from financial assistance should they desire to immigrate; similar restrictions appear to have crept into the selection policies of the other Australian states. Therefore, one major impact of the Leesma organization's activities in London was the spread of Australian xenophobia to embrace other European peoples as well as the feared and despised 'coloured hordes'.

Whether the Western Australian government really believed that the presence of Russian or Jewish Russian immigrants endangered the state's security, or whether it used the August Maren case to mask an Anglo-Saxon distrust of foreign nationals, is not clear. Perhaps the motives were inextricably intertwined, but the fact remains that the unproven statement of a convicted criminal was responsible for modifications in Australian immigration procedures. For the first time these were directed against specific European ethnic groups and automatically subjected all other foreign nationals already resident in Western Australia to investigation if they wished to nominate their families or friends as immigrants to the state. The state government's reaction, when confronted by Ernest Dreger's allegations, was out of all proportion to the degree of danger involved. In a similar though far more serious situation the British authorities had tended towards repression and restriction, but had drawn back after long and painful debate, at least until war lent

114
AFTER-
MATH -
THE ROAD
TO
RESTRIC-
TION

credibility to the sense of emergency. The government of Western Australia, on the other hand, acted precipitously, without even the shortest parliamentary debate on the issue, and the entire Australian handling of the matter illustrates the unreasoning and unsatisfactory grounds that can on occasion trigger such hasty and repressive government action. In this instance, the federal government allowed its concern over immigration expenditure to permit a state to make major alterations in policy in an area constitutionally beyond its competence. In failing to object to the new policies, the federal government effectively endorsed them, not just for use in Western Australia but throughout the Australian Commonwealth.

It remains, finally, to give some details of the lives of the prominent Leesma people. The mystique of Peter the Painter has retained its romantic overtones through the years because no one really knows what befell him once he escaped from London. Was he really an *agent provocateur* for the Ochrana, or was he dedicated and effective operative in the long, secret struggle to overthrow the tsarist regime? There is much to indicate that Peter was a double agent, but his Lettish contemporaries seemed to trust him utterly. Fritz Svaars, who died fighting the British army, was accused by at least one member of Leesma group 5 of being a spy, but Peter, who escaped with suspicious ease, was never doubted.

The unreliable Sergeant Leeson's autobiography gives one account of Peter's subsequent career. Leeson claimed to have received a letter from one of the interpreters employed by the police to translate statements from Russian, Lettish and Yiddish into English. This man, named Casimir Pilenas, claimed that Peter the Painter was his brother, and that he fled finally to America where he died in 1914 in Philadelphia.[18] There was such a person as Peter Pilenas, and one of the informers from the refugee community had already pointed him out to the police in 1911 as Peter the Painter. The police believed otherwise and no action was taken.[19] The informer was mistaken, for Peter Pilenas was already a resident in London's East End when Peter Piaktow was coming to the notice of the French police in Marseilles. Moreover, photographs show that the two men were not identical and bore only a superficial resemblance to one another, rather in the manner of Paul Hubert's likeness to Peter the Painter.[20] Casimir Pilenas obviously sought to bask in the reflected notoriety of Peter the Painter, but his brother, who died in Philadelphia, was not Peter Piaktow.

Richard Deacon, in his history of the British secret service, has made a firm if unsubstantiated assertion that Peter was a successful tsarist agent entrusted with the mission of bringing discredit to the revolutionary cause in Britain, and that he escaped with the connivance of the British authorities and perhaps even the complicity of the Home Secretary.[21] On the other hand, however, Winston Churchill made no secret of his opinion that Peter the Painter 'was one of those wild beasts who, in later years, amid the convulsions of the Great War, were to devour and ravage the Russian State and people'.[22] One of Churchill's recent biographers, Peter De Mendelssohn, has ignored such protestations, and has picked up a suggestion that was current in both the English and Australian newspapers during their discussions of the Houndsditch and the Sidney Street affairs that Peter the Painter was nothing more than a common Russian nickname, a colloquial expression for 'will-o'-the-wisp' or 'Bill Bailey', and that perhaps such an individual never existed outside the imaginations of excited contemporaries.

The police were said to have been keeping an eye on him; but no one seems to have known for certain what he looked like or whether he really was an Anarchist. In fact, one is tempted to wonder whether he actually existed and the police were not perhaps chasing a phantom.[23]

While there is an appealing irony in the possibility that the City of London police were offering £500 reward for the apprehension of a non-existent person, one is forced reluctantly to disagree with De Mendelssohn's thesis. There is too much evidence in favour of Peter's existence for the matter to be so neatly disposed of.

One other writer has offered an explanation of Peter the Painter and his subsequent career, and this account seems to accord approximately with most of the known facts concerning the Houndsditch and Sidney Street affairs, although with a few errors (the account was written fifty years after the events). Moreover, the particulars reported in the memoirs of Eric Pleasants have the added interest of being attributed to Peter Piaktow himself. Eric Pleasants had been captured by the Russians at the end of the Second World War. He had been recruited by the Nazis during the war and was understandably reluctant to return to his own country. A former professional wrestler and circus strongman, he was sentenced to Siberia where he survived privations and adventures worthy of Papillon. At one stage, his guards flung him into a prison cell.

I was gazing up at the ceiling, meditating, when the voice of Pavlov Dudkin brought me back to the prison. He asked me if I was Angleesky Kowalda [the English sledgehammer]. *This was the name given to me by the Russian prisoners. I nodded and he sat on the bed. The only startling thing about Dudkin was his unobtrusiveness; he had been in the same cell with me for a fortnight, and I had hardly noticed him. It was probably this ability to make himself unobtrusive that had made his name a byword to the Russian police, and made him notorious throughout half the world, for Pavlov Dudkin was Peter the Painter, the man who escaped in 1911 from the house in which he and two of his companions had been cornered; they were anarchists who had planned to rob a jeweller's shop in Houndsditch . . .*

116
AFTER-
MATH -
THE ROAD
TO
RESTRIC-
TION

Pavlov looked at me, then said in good English, 'You are a real Englishman?' I nodded, fascinated by this old wrinkled character. 'Well, listen,' said Pavlov, and he began talking in an undertone, with a slight Cockney accent. 'Yes, your English police are efficient and persistent, but you have curious laws in your country which forbid arrest unless there is sufficient evidence of guilt, even then, a man is still considered innocent unless proved guilty; more astounding still, a criminal is given every opportunity to defend himself. If my accomplices had tried to operate in Moscow as we did in London, we would most certainly have been arrested and jailed for life, purely on suspicion. My friends and I were members of the International World Communist Movement. We were disciples of Marx and Engels, one of our leaders was Lenin. We lived a clandestine existence, for nearly all governments had outlawed us, and were wary of our objectives. We had our H.Q. in Paris, and a network of sympathizers that stretched through all the capital cities of Europe. The police in England said we were anarchists. Well, that is a matter of opinion. The only one of our band that could lay any claim to that title was Gardstein, who was courageous to a point of fanaticism. His zeal in our cause had taken him to London.'

'All that time we were desperately short of funds and all means to raise money for the Party were being used. Gardstein had formed a gang of political fanatics and criminals in London. I received a letter from Gardstein telling me of a proposition to raise money for the Party, and I left for London. On arrival, Gardstein introduced me to some of our ardent supporters, several of whom were Russians who had sought political asylum in your country; there was Yourka Duboff, Petropski and Feroleraff. Then two communists from Germany, Josephs and Straus. The remaining members of the gang were crooks from the Continent and England.'

Pavlov Dudkin's story continues through an eerily accurate account of the preparations for the robbery of Harris's jewellery shop, and an allegedly eyewitness description of the murder of the three policemen. He then describes his own escape, and here his story deviates markedly from the account reconstructed in Chapter 2 from the police records.

'I lost no time in making my way to a house of some friends of the Party - a German Jew, called Levi. It was he who had made all the arrangements for the loot to be smuggled abroad. I told him what had happened, and said I must leave the country immediately, for I had reason to believe that the English police knew of my arrival in England, and had been told by the Russian police I was working for a powerful Communist group which was working to undermine the social structure of various countries.'

'We decided to use the arrangements we had made for getting the loot out of the country and to aid my escape. We took a taxi to the

docks where an old tramp steamer was waiting, all papers had been prepared beforehand, the skipper asked no questions. By midday we were well on our way to the Hook of Holland.' [24]

117
AFTER-
MATH -
THE ROAD
TO
RESTRIC-
TION

The story recounted by Eric Pleasants cannot be taken as the last word in the unfinished saga of Peter the Painter. But whether as spy and double agent, or as revolutionary organizer *par excellence*, Peter the Painter continues to exert an historical fascination that has not been matched by many other villains in British history since Jack the Ripper, Dick Turpin or Robin Hood.

The notoriety enjoyed by Peter Piatktow, whose level of participation in the Houndsditch and Sidney Street affrays was at best marginal, is the direct antithesis of the public reputation of Jacob Peters, the man actually responsible for murdering the three unarmed policemen. Even before Fritz Svaars had been killed at Sidney Street, his cousin Jacob Peters had sought to blame him for the entire episode. Whilst awaiting trial in Brixton Prison, Peters continued this policy of turning the recently deceased Fritz into a scapegoat for the attempted burglary and the murders. He informed police and his Social Democratic Party colleagues that he had had nothing to do with either the planning or the perpetration of the crime. He wrote to his party comrades in London and assured them of his innocence. He would never take part in such a risky undertaking, 'because the Political position of the emigrants would be made worse by it'.[25] In a second letter to Lettish Social Democrats in the United States, Peters stated his conviction that the British authorities would eventually be forced to free him once they fully comprehended his guiltlessness in the matter. 'But after all why must I suffer because of my cousin Fritz whom you know, whom Bourlack saw on few occasions. And the same Fritz is the principal accused in the crime, and they took me, his cousin as an accomplice in the crime and on my opinion the whole drama sprung out of that.'[26]

In these attempts to blame the dead man Peters was successful, and he was acquitted of all charges in the Houndsditch murder case, despite the testimony of an eyewitness who saw him carrying the dying George Gardstein and waving a pistol. Peters remained a convinced Social Democrat - the party paid for his defence - and in 1917 he was sent back to Russia as the representative of the London Bolsheviks. From then on his progress was rapid. He quickly gained the goodwill and esteem of men like Lenin and Trotsky, and rose rapidly in the party after the Bolsheviks seized power. During the civil war from 1918-20 he helped organize the dreaded Cheka or political police, and became deputy chairman of the Cheka under the direction of the fanatical Dzerzhinsky. Peters also masterminded the Cheka's armed attack on and extermination of the Black Guards of the Russian anarchists on 13 April 1918. He earned the nickname 'Executioner' because of the number of death warrants he authorized during the following years, and also because he

118

AFTER-
MATH -
THE ROAD
TO
RESTRIC-
TION

was rumoured to have carried out many such executions with his own hands.[27] As the civil war heightened, the Cheka unleashed a red terror in which arrests and executions took place on a massive scale. Jacob Peters was in the thick of it. He continued to prosper in the Cheka after the war and in 1930 was appointed plenipotentiary in Turkestan where he carried out purges of the Red Army. In December 1937 his own turn came, and he was arrested in one of Stalin's purges together with other high-ranking civil and military officers. The date of his execution is unknown, but it is perhaps apt that the man who escaped retribution for shooting three unarmed policemen should eventually die by the same weapon himself. This shabby little murderer, who tried so desperately to blame his own cousin and his Leesma comrades for his crimes, is now officially designated as one of the Soviet Union's 'Heroes of October'.[28]

Karl Hoffman and Luba Milstein's subsequent careers did not attain the heights of power and influence achieved by Jacob Peters. Luba had been Fritz Svaars' mistress, and at the time Fritz was killed, she was in the early stages of pregnancy. Shortly after the Leesma people were acquitted by Mr Justice Grantham, Hoffman and Milstein emigrated to the United States. They remained together for the rest of their lives although they never formalized their relationship by marriage. They dropped out of active politics, and when Luba gave birth to Fritz's son, Karl Hoffman - who was wanted on fifteen or sixteen counts of murder in Russia - found regular employment and supported the family. Fritz's son is today an old-age pensioner in America, and Hoffman and Milstein venerated the memory of the 'great friend' who had been the boy's father. Photographs show Hoffman, Milstein and their two children to have been a normal happy bourgeois family group.[29]

Nina Vasileva's case and subsequent history is perhaps the most difficult to comprehend. She had been abandoned by the Leesma people and it seems likely that her only connection with them had been through her lover, George Gardstein, and her sexual activities with the other males in the group. Once Gardstein was dead, he became a scapegoat for the others, who evidently considered Nina to be similarly expendable. Rudolf Rocker's common-law wife Minnie took Nina under her wing after her release from prison, and Nina lived with the Rockers for several months. She never married and remained for the rest of her life in the East End of London, only a stone's throw from the streets where she had participated in such stirring activities. In the 1960s she was still living in a room by herself, although she was by then in her seventies. The Special Branch kept an eye on her for the rest of her life after 1911.

Sara Trassjonsky ended her days as a lunatic in Colney Hatch Insane Asylum. Her reason never returned after her breakdown caused by the stress of the events preceding her arrest, and she was ruled too ill to be deported.[30]

John Rosen, Osip Federoff and Yourka Duboff made themselves inconspicuous. Shortly before his arrest, Rosen had married his land-

lady's daughter, thereby averting a charge of unlawful carnal knowledge. 119
AFTER-
MATH -
THE ROAD
TO
RESTRIC-
TION His mother-in-law, who had been previously more than anxious to assist the police in linking Rosen with the Leesma terrorists, now suffered a memory lapse and denied her earlier statements. After the Houndsditch trial all three men lived uneventful lives which kept them from coming once more to public attention.

Max Smoller, the sneak-thief who accidentally shot George Gardstein in the back, made good his escape to the continent. He was never heard from again, although the police kept a close watch on the movements of his wife and children. Towards the end of April 1911 Mrs Smoller and her two daughters slipped unobtrusively down to the docks and boarded a ship bound for Bremen. The tickets were purchased under an assumed name, and the woman informed the ship's chief officer that her husband had gone to America and that she and her children intended returning to Russia.[31]

Steinie Morrison, who had claimed to be Australian, and who had been tried and found guilty of the murder of Leon Beron on Clapham Common, was sentenced to death. This was later commuted to life imprisonment. Morrison, like all the people arrested in the course of these events, had no real understanding of the fact that under English law an accessory to a crime was just as guilty as the man actually committing it. There seems little doubt that Morrison had been involved in the killing though he may not have dealt the actual blows. He proved to be a most difficult and intractable prisoner alternating between bitter moroseness and bouts of extraordinary violence. On several occasions he unsuccessfully petitioned the Home Secretary to have the original death sentence carried out. Eventually, he virtually suicided by starving himself to death.[32]

Details in the lives of the immigrants to Australia are also scanty. August Maren changed his name following his release from prison in October 1911, and as Peter Johnson he obtained employment as a public servant with the state government before moving to a position as a commerical traveller in groceries for the Co-operative Stores.[33] He suffered a bout of rheumatic fever which he was later to claim had been brought on by the hardships he had suffered during the months in detention. In 1913 he applied for naturalization as an Australian citizen and the police report made no mention of his early notoriety in England and in Western Australia, commenting merely that he was regarded as 'a very respectable man'.[34] In January 1916 Peter Johnson enlisted in the Australian army and served in the Middle East and on the Western Front for the rest of the war.[35] Peter Johnson had become so embittered by his first experiences in Australia as August Maren that he was to spend the best part of two decades seeking redress from the state government and an admission from the police that they had acted wrongfully in detaining him for so long without trial. In this search for reparations he ultimately enlisted the support of a rising young labour politician named

120

AFTER-
MATH -
THE ROAD
TO
RESTRIC-
TION

John Curtin. Curtin, as editor of the labour paper the *Westralian Worker*, badgered the authorities until he extracted a letter from them which admitted grudgingly that Maren had been held for so long in order to give the English police time to discover whether or not he was Peter the Painter. Curtin described the entire Western Australian episode as a 'monstrous proceeding', and submitted that the local police had been party to a grievous injustice in treating Maren so shamefully.[36] The minister of police reluctantly admitted in January 1927 that Peter Johnson had some legitimate grounds for complaint, but suggested also that the case was now of no interest to anyone but Johnson himself.

In reply to your letter of the 29th December, I have to state that the circumstances in connection with the case of Peter Johnson occurred so long ago, viz. 1911, that it is very probable that few, if any, persons except Johnson himself remember the case. The only reason there was much publicity at the time was because it was alleged that Johnson was identical with the notorious Peter the Painter, who was connected with some crime in London. This aspect was communicated to the CID Scotland Yard, London, and a reply received that it could not be ascertained that he was in any way concerned in the crime in London, and no action was desired by that Department.

Although Johnson was charged with conspiracy, and committed in connection with a case at Doodlakine, it was not proceeded with, and as far as the records show there is nothing against Johnson's character. Not infrequently charges are made against individuals and they are kept in custody until the case is brought on. Even if they are brought to trial and found 'not guilty' no compensation is payable. The case did not even, in this instance, go as far as the charge being proceeded with, which would indicate that the Law Department at that time considered there was not sufficient evidence to sustain any charge. It is regretted that such occurrences take place, and particularly the episode in which Mr Johnson was concerned.

So far as the records of the Police and the Crown Law Department show, there is nothing against Mr Johnson's character.[37]

After the minister's letter August Maren alias Peter Johnson also sinks into anonymity.

August Maren's two friends, Fred Johnson and Peter Older, left even less trace behind them. There is no marriage or death registered for Fred Johnson in Western Australia, nor did he apply for Australian citizenship. There was a file listed in the archives of the Commonwealth Police Force (CRS. A 369) entitled 'Johnson, F. Member of Seamen's and Waterside Workers' Union, Vic. and also suspected Communist', which may have shed some light on Fred Johnson's subsequent Australian career, but unfortunately it has been destroyed. Peter Older remained in Australia and ultimately took out naturalization in 1925. The police report attached to the application briefly notes that there 'is nothing recorded against this applicant'.[38]

121
AFTER-
MATH –
THE ROAD
TO
RESTRIC-
TION

Sufficient information exists about Ernest and Adolf Dreger, and Sarah Ligum for a sketchy outline of their Australian experiences. Ernest Dreger did not make a great deal of money from turning in his former friends to the police. Furthermore, he was robbed of all his worldly possessions when he was arrested and sent to prison. The *Police Gazette* lists the property stolen from Dreger's camp as 'a gentleman's silver open-faced keyless German watch, a gold-coloured curb double chain; a wire strainer; a 10 × 12 tent; a camp oven; a tub and spade; the property of Ernest Dreger'.[39]

Following the completion of August Maren's court case in October 1911, Ernest Dreger and Sarah Ligum married. There is no further mention of either of them until 12 January 1914 when Ernest Dreger applied for naturalization. In conformity with normal procedure in such cases, the commonwealth public service inspector requested a police report on Dreger's suitability for citizenship. It is here that the Western Australian police paid off the debt they owed Ernest Dreger for his co-operation in the case against August Maren. Neither Dreger nor the police mentioned the fact that he was a convicted criminal who had served a gaol sentence for theft. Nor was the Doodlakine episode involving Maren and Johnson referred to. Dreger's statutory declaration and the report submitted by the Western Australian police studiously avoided any reference to the case which had excited such public comment less than three years earlier. It is hard to believe these omissions were not deliberate collusion to ensure Dreger's naturalization. After all, Ernest Dreger's photograph and physical description had been published in the *Police Gazette* shortly after his release from prison in 1911.[40] In no way could it be said that he was unknown to the police, yet the report states,

I respectfully report having interviewed Ernest M. Dreger at Culham. He states that he has no passport and did not receive one when leaving Russia, his explanation being that he was born at Riga, Russia (his parents were German and not naturalized, and the Russian Authorities do not issue passports to persons who have not been naturalized).

Dreger arrived in Bunbury, WA by the SS Garfield as a sailor about five years ago. He deserted the boat at Bunbury and went to work at Kellerberrin for a man named Mackintosh. He had some trouble with some of the other men who were working with him and he left and came to Northam, where he worked for a Miss Dempster for a few months. He then went to Fremantle and after working about there for a month or so went to England, where he stayed for about a year, after which he came out and took up some land at Bayswater, where he resided until he came to Culham some eight months ago.

I made enquiries re his character during the time he has been at

122
AFTER-
MATH -
THE ROAD
TO
RESTRIC-
TION

Culham, and his employer Mr J.H. Phillips states that he has always found him straightforward and honest.

Dreger is a married man and his wife and child are living with him. He speaks English well, but cannot read nor write English.[41]

Ernest Dreger's own statutory declaration stated that he arrived in Western Australia in 1909, that he came out on the *Port Chalmers* and had disembarked at Albany, and that he had resided in the state for five years. It made no mention of the year in England, and seemed intentionally misleading as he listed his locations over the five-year period as: Kellerberrin (1 year 3 months), Bayswater (2 years 9 months), and Culham (1 year). In 1914 he was living at Culham where he had found employment as a labourer.

Adolf Dreger also applied for naturalization at the same time. He also lived at Culham where he worked as a-hairdresser. The whereabouts of William Dreger at this time is unknown, although Ernest's children affirm that the three brothers always kept in close touch with one another. There is no record of any application for citizenship from William Dreger.

In September 1915 Adolf Dreger enlisted in the Australian Army and saw action in the Middle East and on the Western Front where he was wounded in action on three occasions, losing a leg in the final episode of an impressive military career. Ernest Dreger enlisted in the Australian Army in January in 1916 and travelled to the Middle East aboard HMAT *Aeneas* which also carried Peter Johnson (August Maren) to the same destination. There is no record of what the two men had to say to one another, but they both survived the trip. Dreger was later transferred to the Western Front where he was awarded the Military Medal for bravery on 28 January 1918. William Dreger also attempted to join up, but failed his medical examination due to deafness.

After the war Ernest and Sarah Dreger farmed in the Morowa district of Western Australia and reared six children who remember their father as a small, stocky and enormously strong man who, because of his training as a sailor, could run up the side of a water tower or a windmill ladder at a breathtaking speed. His lungs had been affected badly by gas during the First World War, and he died of pneumonia in 1944. Sarah survived him and lived to the age of 81, dying in 1973.

All the Dreger generation who were involved through August Maren with the Leesma organization and the events at Tottenham, Houndsditch, Clapham Common and Sidney Street, are now dead. Their surviving children have no knowledge of Latvian nor any appreciation of the exciting lives led by their parents before coming to Australia. They were never taught the language and culture of their ancestors, and Ernest and Sarah Dreger seemed more than happy to cut off themselves and their descendants from all such contacts with the old country, and to build - like Karl Hoffman and Luba Milstein in the United States - a new life in 'the blessed land of Australia'.

FOOTNOTES

123
AFTER-
MATH -
THE ROAD
TO
RESTRIC-
TION

1   Houndsditch Papers.
2   *The Times*, 4 January 1911.
3   *Hansard Parliamentary Debates*, 4th series, 6 July 1894, vol. 22 col. 83.
4   *The Times*, 7 January 1911.
5   *The Times*, 13 January 1911.
6   *The Times*, 4 January 1911.
7   *The Times*, 13 January 1911.
8   *Report of Inquest on December 20th 1910 and on the 6th January 1911 and the 3rd and 10th days of February 1911, at the City Coroner's Court, concerning the death of Police Sergeant Robert Bentley*, City 1911, no. 26.
9   Robert Anderson, 'The Problem of the Criminal Alien', *Nineteenth Century and After*, vol. 69, no. 408, 1911, pp. 219-24.
10 A.T. Yarwood, *Attitudes to Non-European Immigration*, Melbourne, 1968, pp. 42-3.
11 *The Times*, 21 February 1911.
12 *The Times*, 1 March 1911.
13 Western Australian Police Department file 3911/1911.
14 Myra Willard, *History of the White Australia Policy*, Melbourne, 1923, p. 119.
15 Department of External Affairs CRS A1 Correspondence Files, file 11/10657, Examination of Persons under Immigration Act.
16 Agent General for Western Australia, Correspondence Files, file 1230.
17 Colonial Secretary's Office, Miscellaneous Papers re Immigration, J.S. Battye Library, Perth, WA.
18 Benjamin Leeson, op. cit., p. 223.
19 Houndsditch Papers.
20 Peter Pilenas's photograph appears in William Crocker, *Far From Humdrum*, London, 1967.
21 Richard Deacon, op. cit., pp. 171-3.
22 Winston Churchill, *Thoughts and Adventures*, London, 1932, p. 67.
23 Peter De Mendelssohn, *The Age of Churchill*, London, 1961, p. 506.
24 Eric Pleasants, *I Killed to Live*, London, 1958, pp. 182-7.
25 Houndsditch Papers.
26 ibid.
27 Donald Rumbelow, op. cit., p. 175.
28 See the entry under Peters, Yakov Kristoforovich (1886-1938) in *Who was Who in the USSR*, New Jersey, 1972.
29 Conversation with Donald Rumbelow, 6 May 1979, in which letter and photographs from Karl Hoffman and Luba Milstein's daughter were sighted.
30 Houndsditch Papers.
31 ibid.
32 H. Fletcher Moulton op. cit., pp. xxvii-xxix.
33 Department of External Affairs CRS A1 Correspondence Files, file 13/4526.

124
AFTER-
MATH -
THE ROAD
TO
RESTRIC-
TION

34 ibid.
35 Information from Central Army Records Office, Melbourne.
36 Western Australian Police Department Papers, file 3911/11.
37 ibid.
38 Commonwealth Police Files, Western Australian Commonwealth Archives, file 2685.
39 *Police Gazette*, 6 March 1912.
40 *Police Gazette*, 2 August 1911.
41 Department of External Affairs CRS A1 Correspondence Files, file 14/1043, Dreger, Ernest Mikel.

ROGUES' GALLERY

Dreger, Adolph
Dreger, Ernest Mikel
Dreger, William
Dubof, Yourka (Yourka Laiwin)
Federoff, Osip
Fogel, Jacob (Jan Sprohe, Grishka Sander)
Gardstein, George (P. Morin, Poolka Mourrewitz, Poolka Mourremitz, George Garstin, Schafshi Khan, Yanis Karlowitch Stenzel)
Gershon, Betsy (Gershonova)
Grande, Ougusta ('Quickmate')
Hefeld, Paul ('Elephant')
Hoffman, Karl (Janis Trautman, Chocol, Masais, Peter Trohimtchick)
Johnson, Frederick (George Rosenberg)
Lepidus, Jacob
Ligum, Sarah
Maren, August (Peter Jansen, 'Yahnit', Peter Johnson, John Johnson)
Milstein, Luba
Molchanoff, Pavell (Pavell Molacoff)
Morrison, Steinie (Morris Stein, Stanley Morris, Alexander Petropavloff, Moses Tagger)
Older, Peter
Perelman, Charles
Peters, Jacob (Yakov Peters)
Piaktow, Peter ('Peter the Painter', Peter Schtern, Janis Jaklis, Janis Jakle, Evan Evanovitch Jakle/Jaklis, Serge Makharov ?, Pavlov Dudkin ?)
Rosen, John (John Zelin, 'The Barber')
Sokoloff, William (Joseph)
Smoller, Max (Joe Levi, Marks Smoller)
Svaars, Fritz (Karl Dumnek, Louis Lambert, Peter Trohimtchick)
Tomacoff, Nicholai (Joe Tocmacoff)
Trassjonsky, Sara (Rosa Trassjonsky)
Vanoveitch, Evan (Jan Janoff Palameiko, 'Bifsteks')
Vasileva, Nina (Lena Vassilev)

SELECT BIBLIOGRAPHY

PRIMARY SOURCES

Australian Government, Attorney-General's Department, Correspondence Files.
Australian Government, Department of External Affairs 1, Correspondence Files.
Australian Government, Department of the Interior 1, Correspondence Files.
Australian Government, Prime Minister's Department, Correspondence Files.
Western Australian Government, Colonial Secretary's Office, Registers and Correspondence Files.
Western Australian Government, Police Department, General Personal Files.
Corporation of the City of London, City Police Force, Houndsditch Papers.
Great Britain Government, Metropolitan Police Force, Registers and Files.
Hansard Parliamentary Debates, 1890-1914.

SECONDARY SOURCES

Avrich, Paul, *Anarchists in the Russian Revolution*, London, 1973.
Byrnes, Thomas, *Professional Criminals of America*, New York, 1895.
Chapman, Eddie, *I Killed to Live: The Story of Eric Pleasants as Told to Eddie Chapman*, London, 1957.
Churchill, Randolph S., *Winston S. Churchill*, vol. 2, *Young Statesman 1901-1914*, London, 1967.
Churchill, Winston S., *Thoughts and Adventures*, London, 1932.
Christie, S. and Meltzer, A., *Floodgates of Anarchy*, London, 1970.
Crocker, William C., *Far From Humdrum*, London, 1967.
Deacon, Richard, *A History of the British Secret Service*, London, 1969.
De Mendelssohn, Peter, *The Age of Churchill*, London, 1961.
Dilnot, George, *The Story of Scotland Yard*, London, 1926.
Eddy, J.P., *The Mystery of Peter the Painter: The Story of the Houndsditch Murders, the Siege of Sidney Street and the Hunt for Peter the Painter*, London, 1946.
Fishman, W.J., *East End Jewish Radicals, 1875-1914*, London, 1975.
Fletcher-Moulton, H., 'The Trial of Steinie Morrison', *Notable British Trials*, Edinburgh, 1922.
Futrell, Michael, *Northern Underground: Episodes of Russian Revolutionary Transport and Communications through Scandinavia and Finland*, London, 1963.

Hart, W.C., *Confessions of an Anarchist*, London, 1906.

Hingley, Ronald, *The Russian Secret Police: Muscovite, Imperial Russian and Soviet Political Security Operations 1565-1970*, London, 1970.
Katz, Jacob, *Jews and Freemasons in Europe 1723-1939*, Cambridge, Mass., 1970.
Kebabian, J.S., *The Haymarket Affair and the Trial of the Chicago Anarchists*, New York, 1970.
Kedward, H.R., *The Anarchists: Men who Shocked an Era*, London, 1971.
Kendall, Walter, *The Revolutionary Movement in Britain 1900-21: The Origins of British Communism*, London, 1969.
Kochan, Lionel, *Russia in Revolution 1890-1918*, London, 1966.
Leeson, Benjamin, *Lost London*, London, 1934.
Lindsaar, Peeter, *Eestlased Austraalias ja Uus-Meremaal: Statistiline ja Kronoloogiline Ulevaade*, Sydney, 1961.
Linklater, Eric, *The Corpse on Clapham Common: A Tale of Sixty Years Ago*, London, 1971.
Litvinoff, Emanuel, *A Death out of Season*, London, 1973.
- *Blood on the Snow*. London, 1975.
Lockhart, R.H.B., *Memoirs of a British Agent*, London, 1932.
- *My Europe*, London, 1952.
Macnaghten, Melville, *Days of My Years*, London, 1914.
Nott-Bower, John W., *Fifty-two Years a Policeman*, London, 1926.
Pares, Bernard, *A History of Russia*, London, 1926.
Quail, John, *The Slow Burning Fuse: The Lost History of the British Anarchists*, London, 1978.
Rocker, Rudolf (trans. Joseph Leftwich), *The London Years*, London, 1956.
Rumbelow, Donald, *The Houndsditch Murders and the Siege of Sidney Street*, London, 1973.
Scholz, Heinrich E., Urban, Paul K., Lebed, Andrew I. (eds) *Who Was Who in the USSR*, New Jersey, 1972.
Serge, Victor, *Memoirs of a Revolutionary 1901-1941*, London, 1963.
Seth, Ronald, *The Russian Terrorists: The Story of the Narodniki*, London, 1966.
Sims, George R. (ed.), *Living London: its Work and its Play, its Humour and its Pathos, its Sights and its Scenes*, London, 1906.
Vassilyev, A.T., *The Ochrana; The Russian Secret Police*, London, 1930.
Von Rauch, Georg, *The Baltic States: The Years of Independence 1917-1940*, London, 1974.
Wensley, Frederick, P., *Detective Days: The Record of Forty-Two Years Service in the Criminal Investigation Department*, London, 1931.
Willard, Myra, *History of the White Australia Policy to 1920*, 2nd revised edition, Melbourne, 1967.
Wolin, Simon and Slusser, Robert (eds), *The Soviet Secret Police*, London, 1957.
Yarwood, A. T., *Asian Migration to Australia: The Background to Exclusion 1896-1923*, Melbourne, 1964.
- *Attitudes to Non-European Immigration*, Melbourne, 1968.

INDEX